NOVA SPATIUM SAPIENTIAE

FRESH SENSIBILITIES IN ART AND CULTURE

SARAN S.

ISBN 979-888546658-5

Contents

Contents

Foreword

Dr. Santhosh K.
Principal, University Institute of Technology-Pathiyoor, Associate Professor & HOD (Rtd.)
Department of Sanskrit, KSM DB College, Sasthamcottah, University of Kerala.

Owing to the preponderance of the variety of pedagogical topics on research theories dealt with this catalytic volume titled "Nova Spatium Sapientiae: Fresh Sensibilities in Art and Culture" will ultimately be relished by every genre of Linguistic and literary scholastic community. The multi-faceted analytical framework of the book makes it an immensely readable volume that elaborates the various processes of assimilation. In theme and treatment, every chapter carries an esoteric reflection holding a mirror up to the sparsely delineated issues such as Identity, Geospatial and Digital Humanities, Media and connoisseur ethics, development-oriented planes of communication, Ideological roaming over eco- cultural studies as well as eco-critical investigations, value centred mediations on post-modern narratives fantasy - fiction etc...

Apart from introducing prominent pedagogic linkages that corroborate diverse perspectives such as that of language, writing, evaluation - a compact study on the data analyzing framework also has been meticulously endeavoured in the volume wholesomely. The author outlines explore, defines draws us into the essence of linguistic struggles with issues regarding environment, ethos, habitats and historicity. The volume throws (casts) an ambient aura on rarely attempted linguistic and pedagogic realms such as the stereotypical faiths and ideologies embedded in the postmodern vis-à-vis postcolonial fiction writing. A syllogistic survey on morality, culture and gender roles that are resplendent in the 21st century Neo- Feminism, New -wave cellulosic parameters has been earnestly decoded and deciphered in the pattern of set evaluation, rendering a brilliant exposition.

Moreover, this book provides pathfinding reasons for avid minds that aspire to sharpen their skills in the arena of audio-visual media. A punctilious reference has been rendered on eco-critical studies which is the amalgam of literature and environment from the multidisciplinary as well as interdisciplinary point of view where all sciences appear ‘randomized' to seek out solutions for global issues that threaten sustenance of life and longevity of habitats.

The book could surely be estimated as a beacon light of scholastic reason and pedagogical catechism which could in no way be considered as a cavalcade for cursory perusal. Dabbling into the profound ocean of innovated and updated ideologies, any ambitions diver could emerge from the depths with pearls and emeralds if attempted in a quintessential and dedicated reading mode as Leopold Bloom had suggested.

Since the topics are having intercontinental relevance, the book in every sense stands head and shoulders above its peers regarding the theme, treatment and above all, the sterling information it offers. Ardently scanning the book, an ambitious scholar will undoubtedly have the ecstasy of capturing the iridescence of novel ideas regarding creative notions about the methodology and application of linguistic patterns in Post-modern narrative as well as the Post-Covid Digital era narrative where the cornucopia of Media literacy has opened vast portals for flamboyant writing mandates. My wholehearted cheers for his innovative assay trying to maintain a galaxy of creative and motivational principles radiant in the horizon of pedagogy, by pushing away the clouds of darkness I wish a host of English language aspirants might take his ambitions undertaking a reliable pathfinder.

Editor

Saran S.
Assistant Professor in English
University Extension Centre Pathiyoor
University of Kerala, Thiruvananthapuram.

Saran S. (MA, Ph. D.) is a writer, Poet, Nature Activist, Teacher, and Research Scholar. He has completed his Doctoral Research from the Department of English, M. S. University in 2020. Currently, he is working as an Assistant Professor in the Department of English, University Institute of Technology Pathiyoor, University of Kerala. His areas are Comparative Literature, Cultural Studies, Film Studies, Psychoanalytical Studies and Eco Studies. He is the author of several articles published in various national and international journals as well as six academic books on topics of current interest like English Language, Film Studies, Partition Studies and Cultural Studies. He also authored a collection of poems and short stories. He also edited twenty-one international books. He is the chief editor of Edit Academic, an advisory board member in *The Creative Launcher*, international, open access, peer-reviewed refereed, e-journal in English and also Editorial Board Member in *Shodhkosh: Journal of Visual and Performing Arts* (UGC-Care Listed Journal).

Contributors

1. "Postmodern Reflections in Kamla Markandeya's *Nectar in A Sieve*" - **Dr. Swati A. Sharma**, Professor, Head of Schools, SAGE University Bhopal.

2. "Critical Thinking – A Technique in Enhancing the Skill of Writing Essays at the Under-Graduate Level – A Report" - **Dr. A. Anitha**, Professor, Kalaimagal Arts and Science College

3. "Arvind Adiga's *The White Tiger*: Perspectives on Post-Modernism" - **Dr. Shreeja Tripathi Sharma**, Assistant Professor, Department of English, Institute for Excellence in Higher Education, Bhopal.

4. "Psychopath Don Juan – A Cultural Study of a Mysterious Figure in Both Literary and Practical Context" - **Dr. Gangadevi Sennimalai Marimuthu**, Assistant Professor In English, Department of Foreign Languages, Faculty of Arts And Humanities, Albaha University,, Kingdom of Saudi Arabia.

5. "Phonetics: an Overview" - **Dr. Alok Kumar Singh**, Assistant Professor, Hindi Department, Maa Mansha Devi Mahavidyalaya, Chandauli.

6. "Influence of Social Media in Women in Kerala" - **Dr. Geetha Lakshmi**, Guest Faculty, Bishop Abraham Memorial College, Mallappally, Thuruthicadu, Pathanamthitta, Kerala.

7. "Role of English Language During Pre-Independence and Post-Independence India: A Critical Appraisal" - **Dinesh Kumar**, Assistant Professor in English, Dyal Singh College, Karnal.

8. "General Indian English: A Way Forward" - **Mr. Bhaskara Rao Chintha,** Assistant Professor, Department of

Science and Humanities, St.Martin's Engineering College, Dhulapally, Secunderabad, Telangana.

9. "How ELT Mechanism Works on Differently Abled?" - **Shincy C. Joy,** Ph. D. Research Scholar, SRM University, Andra Pradesh.

10. "New Land Tenure Policy of Travancore and the Beginning of Reclamations in Kuttanadu" - **Nandu.P. Kumar,** Ph. D. Research Schoar, PG and Research Department of History, N.S.S. Hindu College, Perunna, Changanassery, Kerala.

11. "When the People Change the Palace Cannot Hold: A Critical Analysis of the Power by Naomi Alderman" - **Aamina Akhtar**, Research Scholar, Department of English, School of Languages, Linguistics and Indology, Maulana Azad National Urdu University, Hyderabad.

12. "The Surviving Tale of Dalits in Bengal: through the Lens of Survival in my World: Growing up Dalit in Bengal" - **Sutadripa Dutta Choudhury**, Ph. D. Research Scholar, Department of English, St. Xavier's University, Kolkata, India.

13. "The Trauma of Isolation: A Critical Discourse on Sylvia Plath's Poetry" – **Parvathi,** Ph. D. Research Scholar, Department of English, Muslim Arts College, Thiruvithancode, Tamilnadu.

14. "Analysis on Role of Society in Identity Crisis of Transgenders" – **Liji Rose Thomas**

15. "Analysing Covid 19 Pandemic and its Impacts through the Text Lockdown Liaisons" – **Meera Sunny**

Introduction

The word culture comes from the Latin word 'cultura', which means "to occupy, cultivate, or honour." Culture, in general, refers to human activity; various definitions of culture reflect various ideologies or criteria for valuing human effort. The term is now used by anthropologists to indicate the ubiquitous human capacity to classify, encode, and convey experiences symbolically. They consider this ability to be a defining quality of the Homo genus. People living in different places have diverse cultures since culture is learned. Various cultures can exist in different countries, as well as common cultures across continents.

The arts are a broad category of culture that encompasses a wide range of creative undertakings and disciplines. It's a broader term than "art," which normally refers primarily to the visual arts when used to describe a field. Visual arts, literary arts, and performing arts - such as music, theatre, dance, spoken word, and film – are all included in the arts. Art is the manifestation of creativity or imagination in its broadest sense. Art is derived from the Latin word ars, which roughly translates to "order." The act of creating works (or artworks) that utilise the human creative drive and have meaning beyond mere description is usually referred to as art. Crafts and recreational hobby activities are frequently divided from art. The phrase "creative arts" refers to a group of disciplines whose primary goal is to produce material that may be interpreted by the observer or audience. As a result, art can be interpreted in a variety of ways.

Every piece of art that has ever been created has been fueled by inspiration. The source could be happy or sad, real or imagined, or even dredged out from the depths of subconscious intuition at times. Regardless, there is a context. The viewer can choose whether to be interested in learning about the context - whether stylistic, historical, personal, socio-cultural, or political - or simply connect with the product because the work itself is more important. Choosing to observe art with a pristine, uncoloured viewpoint can be refreshing in and of itself, but learning to recognise the subtleties can elevate it to something stunningly spectacular. Its promise may go unrealized if left to its own devices. These questions have been raised by people of all ages, professions, and cultures. Why should a work of art be explained? Is it necessary to assess its technicalities, emotions, and purpose? Is it, in fact, ethical to do so? Are we going against the spirit of the creative process by attempting to explain it to ourselves and the rest of the world?

A more general distinction emerges from a different discourse, inquiring not about the actual effects of the arts but instead about what one might ask of them, whether they should be expected to be useful, or whether the 'art for art's sake' position is right. Although the extreme aestheticism and the kind of formalism defended by Bell, Whistler or Wilde (Lambourne, 2011) might prove hard to sustain, variations on the theme are still current. As we shall see, the intrinsic-instrumental dichotomy has become entrenched in discourses about policy. A more nuanced iteration may be found in Kasser and Ryan's work in psychology, suggesting the ability of the arts and culture to modify value frameworks from one preoccupied with status, income and rewards to one focused on what they present as intrinsic values (Kasser and Ryan, 1996; Kasser 2002; Crompton, 2010). Empirical studies in this area may be relatively recent, but the idea that cultural engagement, as a practice with its internal rewards rather than external monetary or status compensation, may drive intrinsic value orientation has been advocated since the ancient world by philosophers and theorists (Hesmondhalgh, 2014).

Everything and experience in life are inherently questioned, reasoned, liked, or disliked by humans to differing degrees. As with our surroundings, our interactions with art tell a tale that defines us as individuals and socio-cultural beings. Those who are invested in the art for the sake of its intrinsic experience would argue that it makes little difference if the artist was starving, divorced, or a dictator in their role. The aesthetic experience that the visitor has when seeing the piece is more than enough. "Ambiguity is often at the centre of great art," says David Lister, a Fellow of the Royal Society of Arts (2009). Explanation places limitations on the art and limits the viewer's experience, both now and in the future. Respectfully, I must disagree. We don't have to jump right into the artists' explanations of their work as viewers. Allow it to provide insight and perspective. Every work of art becomes more significant in the context of the greater picture when it is placed in context.

CHAPTER I

POSTMODERN REFLECTIONS IN KAMLA MARKANDEYA'S NECTAR IN A SIEVE

Dr. Swati A. Sharma

Professor, Head of Schools, SAGE University Bhopal.

Abstract

Kamla Markandeya is essentially a writer of changing society in India developing under the impact of western influences, physical as well as intellectual and because of social revolution set in by the struggle for independence and the actual freedom that was won in 1947. She treats in her novels the familiar themes but by no means ordinary or common conflict between East and West, industrialization, old feudal values, but hunger and waste and old marital attitudes with a modern sense of freedom. She is also drawn by problems that came in the wake of the movement for women liberation and the continuing domination of manmade society, patriarchal society. She is at her best when painting rural India she lived among the village people to get first-hand knowledge of their life problems and values, she comes across as a sensitive realist novelist of modern India. Kamla Markandeya has a natural affinity for the language she writes in an easy flowing style. Nectar in a Sieve is Kamala Markandeya's first novel. It was first published in 1954 by Messrs Putnam and Co London and subsequently by Jaico publication house Bombay. It was instantly popular and its popularity has been both abiding in its universal appeal to all sections of society not only in

India but also in the western world.

Postmodern Reflections in Kamla Markandeya's *Nectar in a Sieve*

Postmodernism is a broad movement that is defined by an attitude of scepticism, irony, all rejection towards the grand narrative and ideologies associated with modernism. Postmodern thinkers describe knowledge claims and value systems as contingent or socially conditioned, framing them in the political historical and cultural discourse there is a universality of ideas objective reality, morality, truth, human nature and reason. The tendencies to exist in a postmodern world would bring in self-consciousness self-preferential and moral relativism. In its many ways in the writings of Kamla Markandeya, we come to know of the beauty and calm of the countryside and of the peasants engaged in their age-old occupation of tilling the land turning their hair to straw and raising always at the mercy of nature. In drought conditions the family breaks up despite hard work, hunger stalks the land, there are too many mouths to feed on the meagre yield off the small piece of land. Industrialization and modernity have destroyed community life leading to the disintegration of old values and human relationships.

Only the zamindars and the money lenders seem to prosper under these conditions yet amid hunger starvation, destitution, desertion, eviction, prostitution and industrialization, the death of the human spirit occurs. This is also the broad theme of Nectar in a Sieve when illustrated through the trials and tribulations of Rukmini and her husband Nathan. Hunger is a terrible thing it integrates sin demoralises the mere desire to keep alive and makes a desperate man scramble for straws to survive. Irrawaddy is gentle and silent suffering and driven to the extreme because of hunger and starvation, she defies her parents, society, the in-laws and takes up prostitution to feed Kunthi a younger brother who is dying a slow death. Decency loses its meaning when she's trying to appease her hunger and desperation borders on insanity when she is prepared to destroy her former paramour and his family for a handful right of rice, little realizing that she would have to starve even before all of them and starts blackmailing Rukmani.

The title Nectar in the Sieve is taken from Coleridge's famous lines which the novelist has used as the motto for the novel of rural India Work without hope draws nectar in a sieve And hope without an object cannot live. The novel is an enactment of these lines the elixir of immortality, the nectar, the amrita, from the depths of the cosmic ocean. Mount Mandara - a spur of Mount Meru, the world axis—was torn out to use as a churning stick and was steadied at the bottom of the ocean by Vishnu in his avatar (incarnation) as the tortoise Kurma. The asuras held the head of the Naga (half-human, half-cobra) Vasuki, who was procured for a churning rope, and the gods held his tail. When Vasuki's head vomited forth poison that threatened to fall into the ocean and contaminate the amrita, the god Shiva took it and held it in his throat, a feat that turned his throat blue.

The truth has been illustrated through the life story of Rukmani and Nathan enacted against the rural black background this makes the novel a great novel to look at, Markandeya writes that fear hunger and despair are the constant companions of the present fear of the dark future. Fear of the sharpness of hunger fear of the blackness of death, what nectar was to be churned out of the muddied ocean of poverty and misery, where was the cure for the advancing disease of overpopulation or the hopeless veiling of the helpless but the heart that is tempered in the flame of love and faith of suffering and sacrifice will not easily accept defeat. Rukmani the narrator heroine is also a mother of sorrows, she receives shock after aftershock from her husband Nathans infidelity, her dog daughter's sacrifices reaching the streets to save the family from starvation the death of a child Kuti and last the ejection from their house.

Despite their back-breaking work at the farm, they hardly get a square meal a day. Poverty and privations are their life-long companions. The happiness of the Indian farmer depends on the moods of Weather-God. If the weather is favourable, he feels supremely blessed as the rich harvest would enable him to keep the wolf from his door. It arouses hopes in his heart. Rukmani, overjoyed with the hope of rich crop, says, "While the sun shines on you and the fields are green and beautiful to the eyes, and your husband sees beauty in you which no one has seen before and you have a good store of grain laid away for hard times, a roof over you and sweet stirring in your body, what can a woman ask for? My heart sang and my feet were light.

But weather is not always favourable and farmers are well acquainted with its vagaries. The drought or the excessive rain makes the fear of starvation imminent. So much so that a farmer is compelled to sell his possessions like vessels and clothes to pay off the rent. Thus insecurity and privations are part and parcel of the farmer's life. Rukmani tells us, "The calamities of the land belong to it alone, born of wind and rain and weather, immensities not to be tempered by man or his creations. To those who live by land, there must always come a time of hardship, of fear and hunger, even as there are years of plenty. This is one of the truths of our existence, as those who live by the land know.

Rukmani and Nathan face indescribable difficulties and hardships in their peasant life. They are forced to sell their utensils, clothes and even seeds, which hold the prospect for the future crop to pay off their land rent. But they could not save their land and are forcibly deprived of it which compel them to seek refuge at Murugan's home in the city. The sad news of Murugan's desertion of his wife adds to their frustration. They are reduced to the state of mendicants with all their meagre belongings stolen. Trying circumstances compel them to throw themselves upon the resources of the city urchin, Puli. They take up stone-breaking in a quarry outside the city. But they make only a pittance and their lot as urban poor remains as pitiable as their life on the farm. Nathan is completely shattered and dies as a broken man. Rukmani reconciles to her lot and returns with Puli to her native village. Despite so many trials and tribulations, Rukmani retains her motherly love and affection which is expressed in her adopting the leper Puli whom she entrusts to the care of Dr. Kenny.

Kamala Markandaya also shows the evil effects of industrializations followed by urbanization. Industrialization attacks the calm and quiet village life in the form of the tannery. It devours green open spaces, polluting the clean, wholesome atmosphere of the village. The whole village, devoured by the tannery is turned into a spiritual wasteland:

is all noise and crowd everywhere and rude young hooligans are idling in the street and dirty bazaars and uncouth behaviour and no man thinks of another but schemes only for his money. With the establishment of the tannery, an industrial society based on the principle of exploitation comes into existence. It brings the filthy commerce of a town. The death of Rukmani's son, Raja, is compensated with money. It sets all ethical values at nought. Arjun and Thambi clamour for more to eat their fill. Ira whoever had been meek and docile takes up prostitution. Rukmani cries in pain, "Our money buys less and less. As for living in a town if town there is why there is nothing. I would fly sooner from it if I could go back to the sweet quiet of village life. (4)

Soaring prices and greed urge the villagers to demand higher wages. But when their demands are thwarted, they threaten to create trouble for their employers. This has caused menacing tension all over the village. In 'Nectar in a Sieve' Kamala Markandaya highlights the differences between the philosophy of East and West. West in the novel is represented by Dr. Kenny and the tannery. To the west, individuality is the peak and purpose of the whole cosmic process. The westerners think of ego and set themselves against the play of nature. But among Indians, it is fate that finds an important place in man's life. Misfortunes befall a man due to the misdeeds of his previous birth. Indians take them as a punishment from God. When the rain falls, Rukmani like other villagers takes it as God's punishment to them. She tries to propitiate the Goddess with a pumpkin and a few grains of rice. She weeps at her feet in contrition for her sins.

Some of the best Indo Anglian novels written after independence have hunger starvation and the degradation which hunger causes as their theme the finest of these novels in Bhabani Bhattacharya's "So many Hunger" novel deal with a manmade famine off 1942 and the suffering and degradation it causes. Kamla Markandeya's 'Nectar in a Sieve' is another powerful novel that is embraided with the theme of poverty and hunger, it is established in a rural setting and the hunger and starvation are caused by the operation of natural forces, excessive rains or utter drought. The central figures against heavy odds raise the novel to lofty heights of an epic, it is a novel of ethical dimensions like the Good Earth this first novel of India recalls in its savage power an authentic atmosphere the greatness of the Chinese novel the good earth it records vividly the poverty-stricken heart-breaking existence of poor tenant farmers of Madras but in its particular theme the story of Rukmani her husband and children.

There is a universality of love and loyalty that will appeal to the readers all over the world Rukmani the heroine narrator of the story is married to a poor tenant farmer Nathan despite their poverty they live happily in their small mud house they are content but suddenly the misfortunes come upon them in quick succession a number of children doctor era and six sons I born to them in quick succession the supply of food and so many mouths to feed render them unsuccessful the great tragedy of era Bing Baron and is thrown out by the husband is born silently then a tannery is constructed on the outskirts off the village and it makes the Nathan family disintegrate prices rise there is increased ugliness and wickedness two of their sons Arjun and Thambi take up service in the tannery then they are terminated after a strike and they go away far to live in Ceylon and Rukmini in Nathan here of them no longer Raja another son goes to the tannery Anne is caught stealing a large piece of skin he's killed by the lucky blows and his dead body is brought to Rukmani who resigns to the greatest loss.

Rukmini India wars the loss with hero IK common resignation there is no protest no loud lamentation butter pregnant and heart rending grief is conveyed for this I have given you birth my son that you should lie in the end at my feet with ashes in your face and coldness in your limbs and yourself departed without trace leaving this huddle of bones and flash without meaning already I think the eyes must be closed the death has glaze them and I do so the joy must we died for it is sagging I put a bandage about it the body must be washed and I wash it an error comes to help and cleanses the mouth which I had forgotten to do these things were you now there is a connection whatever the sorrow within me is not for this body which has suffered end in suffering has let slip the spirit what for you my son it is almost like the morning of an epic hero killed in action Murugan another son also leaves them and goes to the city to take up service there therefore sons I've gone away in quick succession causing great grief and suffering to their parents. (5)

This beautiful and eloquent story tells of a simple peasant woman in a primitive village in India whose whole life was a gallant and persistent battle to care for those she loved. Married as a child bride to a tenant farmer she had never seen, she worked side by side in the field with her husband to wrest a living from land that was ravaged by droughts, monsoons, and insects. With remarkable fortitude and courage, she sought to meet changing times and fight poverty and disaster. She saw one of her infants die from starvation, her daughter becomes a prostitute, and her sons leave the land for jobs that she distrusted. And somehow, she survived.

There are so many stories that highlight India's life right after the independence but only a few stand out. Nectar in a Sieve is one such groundbreaking classic Indian literature that brings out the basic and simple life of a farmer somewhere rural in South India. Centralizing poverty as the main theme of the book, the author had depicted the life of a village woman whose sadness knew no limit, she had a fulfilling and satisfying family life with limited happiness and extreme challenges throughout her way. The author has made her readers feel nostalgia through the pages of this compelling yet heart touching story of a woman as a little girl, as a daughter, as a wife, as a mother and as a friend as she survives her life alongside her husband and children.

The author has captured the backdrop of a post-Independent India strikingly as she gracefully painted the rough and brown yet dull landscape of an Indian village, lush with rice paddy fields and the blooming flora here and there, the dust from the red stone roads, the greyish river, the hard cracked soil, the mud huts, the narrow-minded and illiterate village folks, the superstitions, the child's cry, the staple food, and the sweat of the hard-working villagers. Every detail about the background image will let the readers time travel back and forth from that era to the modern times and that will force them to reflect on the changes. The author had also highlighted the socio-political, cultural norms and beliefs followed back in that era which is in stark contrast to present day's rules and beliefs.

The author's writing style is extremely significant rich with emotions and wisdom embedded deep into the core of the storyline. The readers, be they international or Indian, will find the book easy to comprehend with even the story is written by the author is very simple and easy to understand the English language. The narrative is heartfelt and articulate and the readers will find themselves losing themselves in the sad undertone of the character's voices. The pace of the book is swift and moderate even the story is rich with so many evocative descriptions that will help the readers to not only feel the story but also to visually imagine the scenes right before their eyes.

The characters reflect the hardships toiled by the Indian farmers and their families through their honest and realistic demeanour strikingly. The main character of Rukmani is pleasingly portrayed that the Indian readers can easily contemplate with her plain looks, not so sharp wit, an enduring and patient woman, a hard-working mother, a loyal and devoted wife and an obedient daughter. Rukmani infers poignancy and sympathy through her painful journey of life in India, how motherhood and marital life changes the life of this once innocent and sweet little girl is equally heartbreaking yet enlightening enough to keep the readers glued to the pages of this book till the very end. the supporting characters are well developed and extremely enriching enough to keep the readers interested in the way their life unfolds through the main storyline.

Rukmani has been taught to bear sorrow in silence. She believes sorrow is a chastening process, she remains stoic in the face of vicissitudes of life. She believes that nothing is unbearable and man's undaunted and indomitable spirit helps him to overcome all trials and tribulations by endurance. She patiently endures the vagaries of her life and waits for the times to be better. Her passive acceptance of her misfortune and sanguineness about the time to come irks Dr Kenny who chides her saying, "Times are better, times are better".

Times will not be better for many months. Meanwhile, you will suffer and die. You meek suffering fools! why do you keep this ghastly silence? He believes that instead of enduring the things patiently man must fight against that heavy odd for his survival. The village huts are uprooted in the storm while the tannery withstands the onslaughts suggesting that the western rationality has the timber to survive, to fight the heavy odds. Nevertheless, westerner Kenny fails to save his marriage from breaking down. On the contrary, Rukmani believes that man's spirit has strength enough "to rise above his misfortune" She knows that all wants cannot be fulfilled, "Want is our companion from birth to death, familiar as the seasons of the earth, varying only in degree what profit to bewail that which has always been and cannot change" (8).

Not only Rukmani but old Granny too has become used to bearing misfortune with courage and fortitude. She lives alone making a meagre living by selling vegetables. Western philosophy is rational, scientific and materialistic. It advocates for a certain amount of planning about the future. But Rukmani cannot plan, "How can we? It is not within our means. We are in God's hands" (8). She has firm faith in God and draws from it the strength to surmount all difficulties. She is deeply rooted in traditionalism. Though she accepts western science to cure Puli of his leprosy, she does not accept it beyond that. Unable to appreciate each other's behaviour, Rukmani and Kenny nevertheless remain friendly with each other.

Kamala Markandaya also draws our attention to human relationships, the way they are formed, sustained and disintegrated. The central characters, Rukmani and Nathan prize their relationship above everything. It is their harmonious conjugal bonds that give them strength to bear the buffets of cruel nature and corrupting influence of the ugly industrialization. Despair, disappointments and frustration abound their life but they endure them bravely like the true heroes and feel happy in each other's company. When Nathan while lying on the death - bed, asks Rukmani,

Have we not been happy together?" "Always my dearest always", says Rukmani. Rukmani, the youngest daughter of the village headman, due to the poor economic conditions of her father, is married to Nathan, a tenant farmer. She soon reconciles to her fate because she finds Nathan 'poor in everything but in love and cares for his wife. She lives with Nathan facing utter penury, privations and hardships courageously. Mutual love and understanding characterise their conjugal bonds. Rukmani feels Nathan be with her even after his death. (12)

The novel opens with Rukmani telling the readers, "Sometimes at night I think that my husband is with me, coming gently through the mist and we are tranquil together. Then morning comes, the wavering turns to gold, there is a stirring within as the sleepers awake and he softly departs" (15). Nathan's love and care for his wife do not let his landless status and limited financial resources come in the way of their happiness. He shows great patience towards his ignorant, plain child bride, who imbibes many household jobs from Kali and Janaki. He is aware of Rukmani's deep anguish and disappointment on seeing his mud-hut. He knows that she is used to better living and makes a sincere effort to cheer her up, assuring her of the better times to come. His loving concern and good conduct win Rukmani's heart. He says to Rukmani with a pleading look, "Perhaps you are frightened at living here alone - but in a few years we can move - maybe even buy a house such as your father's. You could like that?" (15).

Nathan loves Rukmani immensely so he builds his huts with his own hands for the welcome of his bride. Rukmani's heart is filled with joy at the thought of having a loving and considerate husband. Nathan too is equally happy with

Rukmani whom he considers the best of all women. On Diwali day when they enjoy themselves around the bonfire, Nathan lifts her and says, "I am happy because life is good and children are good and you are the best of all" There are occasions when Nathan loses his temper and uses harsh words. But even in anger, he is never inconsiderate towards Rukmani. When he is unable to collect the required amount to pay to the landlord, he decides to sell everything including the seeds for the next crop. Rukmani does not acquiesce. Nathan angrily says, "Do you think I am blind and do not see or so stupid as to believe that crops are raised without seeds? Do you take me for a fool?" (16).

Rukmani knows that 'It was due to the terrible choice forced upon us and he never meant to be harsh'. Though they are devoted to each other, yet there have been aberrations in their lives. Nathan was drawn towards Kunthi and sired her two sons. Hence he always remains fearful lest Kunthi should divulge the secret of his illicit relationship with her to Rukmani. But eventually, he has to confess his sin to Rukmani when the latter reproaches the children for stealing rice. On learning about Nathan's moral lapse, she is deeply anguished and feels cheated. But she does not give vent to her anguish as she has concealed from Nathan her relationship with Kenny whose medical assistance helps her bear a son and cures Ira of her barrenness. But she does not want her husband to know it because being a foreigner Dr Kenny is dubbed as being with the rulers and oppressors. She meets Kenny surreptitiously because as she is 'sure Nathan would not like his wife or his daughter going to a Whiteman, a foreigner'.

Like Nathan Rukmani too has been blackmailed by Kunthi, who extracted rice from her for not divulging Nathan of her going to Dr. Kenny. Rukmani thinks Nathan to be her most precious possession and does not want to lose her, "I need you", I cried to myself, 'Nathan my husband I cannot take the risk, because there is a risk since she is clever and I am not. She tells Nathan that Kunthi extorted rice from her also and feels much relieved because now she was 'freed from the necessity for lies and concealment and deceit with the fear of betrayal. The conjugal relationship between Rukmani and Nathan is strong enough not to be disrupted by this unpleasant episode. It provides the strength to bear with stoic calm immense suffering caused by industrialization and deprivation of their land. Their relationship is based on mutual trust, faith and understanding.

Conclusion

The Postmodern elements in the 'Nectar in a Sieve' may sound predictable-rural forbearance in the face of industrialization-but the novel did not succumb to cliché. On the contrary, the protagonist's "voice" can sometimes seem a little too cosmopolitan to fit into her context. Markandaya, of course, rejected criticism that her characters were not fully "there": "The fundamental mistake," she argued, "is to think that a peasant thinks differently from you." Yet, the novel has its peculiarities, when villagers talk of "fried pancakes" and "rice cakes" to avoid words like pakoras and idlis. She won adulation for presenting India to the world, but to many Indians, this came at the cost of genuine "Indianness". Markandaya had moved to London and married an Englishman. Her later life informed the inter-racial, East-West dynamics that animate her novels. After memorable works that reflect on faith and reason, hope, frustration and more in urban India, when Markandaya tried to break away from what was expected of her, she did not find support forthcoming. As long as she played the role charted for her as a storyteller of India, it seemed, she was welcome, but a commentary on the West would not be easily digested.

This, then, became the tragedy of Markandaya. She was gifted and possessed both skill and perspective, but over time there was "a slow decline in her reputation as a writer that finally dwindled to silence". The West, where she won the principal share of her appreciation, moved on in the 1980s to a new generation with new approaches, while her motherland in the East thought her de-Indianized and out of touch. Her characters were, as Ezekiel put it, mere "puppets, manufactured for those who know nothing about India". But all said and done Markandaya told India's tales to the world beyond, and brought a young, new nation into the global literary conversation.

Works Cited

Barr, Donald, "To a Modest Triumph," in New York Times Book Review, March 15, 1955, p. 4.

Dunlea, William, "Tale of India," in Commonwealth, Vol. LXII, No. 20, August 19, 1955, pp. 500-501.

Glencoe Literature Library, Study Guide for Nectar in a Sieve by Kamala Markandaya, http://www.glencoe.com/sec/literature/litlibrary/pdf/nectar_in_a_sieve.pdf (last accessed July, 2021).

"Kamala (Purnaiya) Taylor," in Contemporary Authors Online, The Gale Group, 2001.

Muehl, J. F., Review of Nectar in a Sieve, in Saturday Review, May 14, 1955.

"Overview: Nectar in a Sieve, by Kamala Markandaya," Literature Resource Center, The Gale Group, 1999.

South Dakota School of Mines and Technology Study Guide: South Asia Reading Series, Fall 1998, http://www.sdsmt.edu/online-courses/is/hum375/

southasia.html (last accessed July, 2021).

Teacher's Guide: Nectar in a Sieve by Kamala Markandaya, http://www.penguinclassics.com/US/resources/teachers_guides/t_markandaya_nectar.html (last accessed July, 2021).

Walsh, William, "Markandaya, Kamala," in Contemporary Novelists, 6th ed., St. James Press, 1996, pp. 653-54.

Bhatnagar, Anil K., Kamala Markandaya: A Thematic Study, Sarup & Sons, 1995.

Lalita, K., and Susie J. Tharu, eds., Women Writing in India, Feminist Press at the City University of New York, 1991.

Parameswaran, Uma, Kamala Markandaya, Rawat, 2000.

Rao, A. V. Krishna, Kamala Markandaya: A Critical Study of Her Novels, 1954–1982, B. R. Publishing Corporation, 1997

CHAPTER II

CRITICAL THINKING – A TECHNIQUE IN ENHANCING THE SKILL OF WRITING ESSAYS AT THE UNDER-GRADUATE LEVEL – A REPORT

Dr. A. Anitha

Professor, Kalaimagal Arts and Science College

Abstract

Of the four language skills, writing is the most complex and difficult one. There are numerous problems in our context which work against the teaching writing skills. This article describes how Dictogloss, an integrated activity, helps to teach writing effectively. This activity is based on the interactive approach which is a learner-centred one. The learners also get practice in all the four skills – Listening, Speaking, Reading and Writing. Beginning with an introduction to teach writing skills and its aim the paper presents the problem of teaching writing from the perspectives of teachers, learners and administrators. The four approaches to teaching writing and the procedure of Dictogloss and the objectives, that is teaching writing through listening, speaking and reading using Dictogloss then follows. Finally, the importance of Dictogloss and the conclusion has arrived.

Background

It is impossible to write anything without some amount of prior thinking. This becomes more applicable to the students of the English language classroom, both in ESL and EFL. Most current theoretical approaches and practical demands from the students and the teachers' goals hover around making learners automatic, automated and autonomous miracle workers with the English language. In this rush, one of the rescues comes from the techniques in 'Critical Thinking'. Thinking in isolation can degenerate to mere daydreaming and progress to random flashes at the most in an ELT classroom. Paul and Linda observe, "Everyone thinks; it is our nature to do so. But much of our thinking, left to itself, is biased, distorted, partial, uninformed or down-right prejudiced. Yet the quality of our life and that of what we produce, make, or build depends precisely on the quality of our thought. Shoddy thinking is costly, both in money and in quality of life. Excellence in thought, however, must be systematically cultivated," (Richard Paul and Linda Elder, 2008).

In a seminal study on critical thinking and education in 1941, Edward Glaser defines critical thinking as follows "The ability to think critically, as conceived in this volume, involves three things: (1) an attitude of being disposed to consider in a thoughtful way the problems and subjects that come within the range of one's experiences, (2) knowledge of the methods of logical inquiry and reasoning, and (3) some skill in applying those methods. Critical thinking calls for a persistent effort to examine any belief or supposed form of knowledge in the light of the evidence that supports it and the further conclusions to which it tends. It also generally requires the ability to recognize problems, to find workable means for meeting those problems, to gather and marshal pertinent information, to recognize unstated assumptions and values, to comprehend and use language with accuracy, clarity, and determination, to interpret data, to appraise evidence and evaluate arguments, to recognise the existence (or non-existence) of the logical relationship between propositions, to draw warranted conclusions and generalizations at which one arrives, to reconstruct one's patterns of beliefs on the basis of wider experience, and to render accurate judgements about specific things and qualities in everyday life.

But given the amount of time that a teacher gets with her students in today's timetable and the demands placed on her, she cannot in any possibility take chances with her students. Mere thinking will have to be coupled with reason and a proper critique of the thinking process itself. Thus emerges the concept of Critical Thinking in the Indian classroom. The term has been in broad use perpetually in all walks of one's life but in its incipient state. A cultivated form becomes a wonderful tool in the hands of the teacher. Critical thinking is as much a developable skill as language learning. Both when engaged together work harmoniously with each other. Thus, Critical Thinking can become an integral part of English Language Teaching and Learning. It has the capacity to contribute positively to the learner-centric demands of the stakeholders. This, when used as a technique matures into the much-needed learner autonomy. The paper discusses the use of 'Critical Thinking' as a technique to teach essay writing at the undergraduate level.

Definition of Critical Thinking used in this paper:

Critical thinking is a mode of thinking on any topic, content, or problem – in which the thinker uses quality thinking while skillfully analysing, assessing, including or excluding and reconstructing ideas in order to effectively communicate and to overcome egocentrism and socio-centrism in a mixed ability ELT classroom.

Aim:

To enable the students to effectively use some of the critical thinking strategies as tools while they are working with a general topic and broadly associated ideas just before they actually write an essay on the topic.

Assumptions:

1. The students are familiar with the topic of the essay arrived at after due discussion.
2. The teacher has a firm grounding in Critical Thinking.

Materials:

Intellectual: Strategy List: 35 Dimensions of Critical Thought, topics on which essays are to be written, associated ideas.

Physical: Blackboard, chalk and furniture to facilitate free student movement in the classroom.

Students: 40 in number from semester 1 of the Under Graduate Students' programme.

Time: 120 minutes

Method:

Step 1: The topic of the essay was finalised and written on the blackboard and the students were asked to spell out ideas that could be used while writing the essay. Every idea was accepted and written on the blackboard, none discarded. (10 minutes)

Step 2: The students were given the 35 strategies list (annexure) and were allowed to skim through it. (5 minutes)

Step 3: Now the teacher put them in pairs and asked them to discuss the ideas that can become a part of the essay first individually and the students discussed with the partners their choice of ideas and the reason for doing it. The students were also engaged in building a skeleton of the essay and organised the ideas into possible paragraphs. The students were encouraged to carefully study their thinking process and take support from the list to aid them in the explanation to their partners. (15 minutes)

Step 4: The pairs were collapsed into groups of four in a random fashion and continued their discussion while justifying their choices to the other members of the group. In a cascade fashion, the groups were collapsed till they formed a single large group. (60 minutes)

Step 5: The teacher allowed the students that slightly differed in their choices to voice out and convince the class. Differences in opinions of about 20% were considered normal and accepted by the teacher as long as they were able to justify their choice from the strategy list. (10-20 minutes)

Step 6: The students wrote their choice of ideas in a justified and reasoned manner and were ready to submit/ write their essays in the next class.

Throughout the class, the teacher played the role of a facilitator in the background.

Results:

The students were able to positively engage in conversation and discussion with their class and voted this method as one of the better ways of preparing to write essays. Mind mapping was converted into informed choice and organization of ideas.

Evaluation:

Merits:

1. All the students had equal opportunities to participate in the process and they did participate.
2. Disorganised thinking was given a proper, justified and informed direction that got the students thinking about

their thinking process while they worked on the choices.

3. This technique brought in a sense of variety into the classroom and the students felt important while they were involved in the activity.
4. The teacher found yet another technique to get the students talking to themselves, to their classmates and to the entire class.
5. The skills acquired here are transferable to other similar and dissimilar situations.
6. The differing opinion clashes are rated as opinion clashes and the students learn to understand and respect each other.
7. All the three (Bloom) domains of the individual were engaged by the end of the class.

Limitations:

1. It became difficult to read and get palpable results of the thinking process right away.
2. The classroom got out of control sometimes.
3. Some students found it difficult to understand some strategies.

Handling Limitations:

1. The results of the right-thinking processes were read by gauging the response given by the students and the teacher facilitated and put the thinking process on track wherever it detailed. The teacher sent the students back to the 35-strategy list.
2. The teacher intervened and made peace between the students and accepted the deviations and arguments in

a healthy manner and encouraged the students to repeat the strategy.

3. The teacher explained in detail the problematic strategies to these students.

Conclusion:

The topic of the essay becomes the 'problem' and the students are encouraged to become critical thinkers to use quality thinking to skillfully analyse, assess, include or exclude and reconstruct ideas. This strategy helps overcome egocentrism and socio-centrism in a mixed ability ELT classroom.

The scope of the paper is limited to 'preparation to write' – mind- mapping, collection of ideas, organization and such activities. It is workable and possible to include Critical Thinking in practical contexts elsewhere in the undergraduate classrooms while aiming to make it a habit. The results that are based on an experiment tried out on the undergraduate students of the Anna University prove that it contributes to learner autonomy. The broad theoretical framework of the paper is drawn from the Critical Thinking Society and related critical thoughts and discussions on the areas.

The technique involved students being aware of the strategies of Critical Thinking and applying the relevant ones in activities; individual, pair and group. This technique is different from the routine preparation to write in the sense that in critical thinking the preparation is more focussed, analytical and informed. The technique enhanced the process of learning to write and contributed positively to the preparation to write essays.

Strategy List: 35 Dimensions of Critical Thought Formally Named

We have broken the global concept of critical thinking down into 35 aspects or instructional strategies.

A. Affective Strategies (related to your heart)

- S- 1 thinking independently
- S- 2 developing insight into egocentricity or sociocentricity
- S- 3 exercising fairmindedness
- S- 4 exploring thoughts underlying feelings and feelings underlying thoughts
- S- 5 developing intellectual humility and suspending judgement
- S- 6 developing intellectual courage
- S- 7 developing intellectual good faith or integrity
- S- 8 developing intellectual perseverance
- S- 9 developing confidence in reason

B. Cognitive Strategies – Macro-Abilities (related to your mind -1)

- S- 10 refining generalizations and avoiding oversimplifications
- S- 11 comparing analogous situations: transferring insights to new contexts
- S- 12 developing one's perspective: creating or exploring beliefs, arguments, or theories
- S- 13 clarifying issues, conclusions, or beliefs
- S- 14 clarifying and analysing the meaning of words or phrases
- S- 15 developing criteria for evaluation: clarifying values and standards
- S- 16 evaluating the credibility of sources of information

- S- 17 questioning deeply: raising and pursuing root or significant questions
- S- 18 analysing or evaluating arguments, interpretations, beliefs, or theories
- S- 19 generating or assessing solutions
- S- 20 analysing or evaluating actions or policies
- S- 21 reading critically: clarifying or critiquing texts
- S- 22 listening critically: the art of silent dialogue
- S- 23 making interdisciplinary connections
- S- 24 practising Socratic discussion: clarifying and questioning beliefs, theories, or perspectives
- S- 25 reasoning dialogically: comparing perspectives, interpretations, or theories
- S- 26 reasoning dialectically: evaluating perspectives, interpretations, or theories

C. Cognitive Strategies – Micro- Skills (related to your mind – 2)

- S- 27 comparing and contrasting ideals with actual practice
- S- 28 thinking precisely about thinking: using critical vocabulary
- S- 29 noting significant similarities and differences
- S- 30 examining or evaluating assumptions
- S- 31 distinguishing relevant from irrelevant facts
- S- 32 making plausible inferences, predictions, or interpretations
- S- 33 giving reasons and evaluating evidence and alleged facts
- S- 34 recognizing contradictions
- S- 35 exploring implications and consequences

Works Cited

Edward M. Glaser, An Experiment in the Development of Critical Thinking, Teacher's College, Columbia University, 1941.

Richard Paul and Linda Elder, The Miniature Guide to Critical Thinking Concepts and Tools, Foundation for Critical Thinking Press, 2008.

"Strategy List: 35 Dimensions of Critical Thought Formally Named"

http:// www.criticalthinking.org/page.cfm?Page ID = 466& Category ID = 63

Bio-Note

Name: **Dr. A. Anitha**

Designation: Professor

College: Kalaimagal Arts and Science College

Experience: 19 Years

Area of Interest: English Language Teaching, Rebel Literature, Afro- American Literature and Indian Literature.

CHAPTER III

ARVIND ADIGA'S THE WHITE TIGER: PERSPECTIVES ON POST-MODERNISM

Dr. Shreeja Tripathi Sharma

Assistant Professor, Department of English

Institute for Excellence in Higher Education, Bhopal.

ABSTRACT

Post-Modernism connotes the epistemological critique which shatters the prevalent unquestionable belief in morality and rationality. The movement sustains a renaissance of the scepticism associated with constant questioning of the already existing values and ideologies. This research paper explores Arvind Adiga's novel, *The White Tiger*, from a post-modern lens particularly concerning anti-totalization, decentralisation and disruptive societal structure. The novel vehemently rejects the established social order and questions the validity of right and wrong, good and bad, ethical and unethical. The novel evokes multiple facets of Postmodernism and mirrors the lack of fixity of any kind in our lives in the post-modern age.

Keywords: Arvind Adiga, White Tiger and Post-Modernism

• • •

Arvind Adiga's *The White Tiger*: Perspectives on Post-Modernism

Postmodernism connotes the renaissance of cynical, sceptical thought processes marked by a constant questioning of the existing values, structures of authority and ideologies. The movement symbolises an epistemological critique that shatters the prevalent belief in the unquestionable notion of ideas such as morality and rationality. It boldly rejects any possibility or need of principles based on verifiability and homogeneity. The movement intensely argues against the existence of standards such as right and wrong; good and bad; ethical and unethical. It sanctions actions determined not by logic, rationality or by the approved norms of the society; but by individual considerations and needs. Change and disorder thus become welcome forces of the post-modern world. The association, allegiance or reverence towards any form of a universally stable pattern or structure is vehemently disregarded. The postmodern movement stirred in the 1960s in the West with the emergence of post-industrialization and consumerism. The period was marked with several socio-economic by-products such as globalisation and multiculturalism, the spread of information technology, mass media and the 'knowledge' industries. The period signifies a retreat from colonialism and utopianism as well as the rise of a new identity in terms of politics, ideology, race and gender.

It gradually created a wave of disillusionment with Enlightenment and postEnlightenment rationalist ideas about the unity of the self and belief in ideals such as universal justice. The term was used in a literary context to describe new kinds of experimental literature arising out of but moving beyond, the terms of aesthetic modernism. The question of defining post-modernism becomes complex in terms of overlapping interlinkages between modernism and post-modernism. It is debatable whether –postmodernism proclaims modernism, or reupdates, or obscures or surpasses modernism. However, a general accord holds that modernism itself is inevitably postmodern, in its ever transitional contemporaneity and its relevance to the immediate present. Exploring the marginalized aspects of life and society is a fundamental concern of postmodernism. Postmodernism is typically characterised by refuting pre-fixes like - 'dis', 'de', 'in' and 'anti' which project it as a process of differing which subverts, the very concept it seeks to define. The movement creates an array of 'little narratives' as well as a broader epistemic sense of crisis as an elemental part of the discourse. Arvind Adiga's *The White Tiger* presents typical features of postmodernism through its portrayal of the underdogs in the wake of emerging consumerism in India. Adiga exposes the unstable base of the social pyramid of Indian society which inevitably attracts a disruption of the totalitarian super-structure. The pathetic socio-economic status of the poor men at the base and their yearning to climb the ladder of success to bring an end to their sufferings becomes the driving force of disruption.

The novel captures a slice of postmodern plight through its protagonist BalramHalwai. The novel is set in an economically bourgeoning modern India, when the Indian government adopted a policy of economic liberalization, after a phase of bankruptcy in 1991, which forced the country to take a major loan from the International Monetary Fund. The policy resulted in a high rate of economic growth and foreign investment which continues to the present day. However, the economic boom also drastically increased income inequality. The novel addresses the concerns of ' half-baked' masses like Balram and destabilizes the discourse into a stupor of postmodern disruption. The novel is written in an epistolary form comprising of seven letters written to Wen Jiabao, The Premier of China, who is visiting India to address entrepreneurs of India. Balram Halwai, informs him about the reality behind India's so-projected "world's biggest economy" image. Balram shares the story of his metamorphosis from a servant at a teashop in Laxmangarh into an entrepreneur while revealing the stark reality of income inequality in India's industrial expansion and explores the class struggle in India during a time of modernization and globalization.

Adiga compares the Indian socio-economic reality with the 'rooster coop' packed with birds of numerous kinds who witness their comrades being slaughtered but do not have the courage or understanding to rebel against the atrocious, dogmatic totalitarian superstructure. Balram realises that the metaphorical coop is more of an internal metal conditioning rather than an external social structure. As the novel progresses the protagonist Balram metaphorically breaks free from the 'rooster coop' and transforms as the 'White Tiger' in a post-modern context. He captures the subservient mentality of the Indian base structure and writes:

Every day, on the roads of Delhi, some chauffeur is driving an empty car with a black suitcase sitting on the back seat. Inside that suitcase is a million, two million rupees; more money than that chauffeur will see in his lifetime. If he took the money he could go to America, Australia, anywhere and start a new life. He could go inside the five-star hotels he has dreamed about all his life and only seen from the outside. He could take his family to Goa, to England. Yet he takes that black suitcase where his master wants. He puts it down where he is meant to, and never touches a rupee. Why? Because Indians are the world's most honest people, like the prime minister's booklet will inform you? No. It's because 99.9 percent of us are caught in the Rooster Coop just like those poor guys in the poultry market" (Adiga, 175).

The novel subverts the established axiom of the man's journey from darkness to light through Balram's paradoxical narrative. As he progresses through the social order, Balram considers his apparent progression as a journey from darkness to light. However, in a typically post-modern context, it soon becomes evident that the light that he begets is bleaker than the darkness. As the novel progresses Balram murders his master Mr. Ashok and takes away his money to start a business as an entrepreneur. He breaks the 'rooster coop' and finds wings to proclaim his freedom. However, he fails to realize that on breaking one coop he enters another which is stronger and more elusive. The possibility of redemption in a post-modern world appears to be an alluring trap, a vicious circle escape from seems impossible. Balram associates his freedom with chandeliers, beautifully emanating light. But the light they emanate is as artificial as the freedom he begets by acquiring wealth. He compares his freedom paradoxically with the idea of liberation which his mother attained after her 5 death and her funeral rites in the holy Ganga.

During the funeral of his mother on the banks of Ganga in Benaras, he ironically feels that the black mud of Ganga was not liberating but something that was "holding her back" from liberation: She was trying to fight the black mud; her toes were flexed and resisting, but the mud was sucking her in.... And then I understood: this was the real god of Benaras- this black mud of the Ganga into which everything died, and decomposed, and was reborn from, and died into again. The same would happen to me when I died and they brought me here. Nothing would get liberated here" (Adiga,18). The novel posits the idea that the postmodern world is ruled by materialism and capitalism much like the black mud on the banks. Balram belongs to Laxmangarh in the district of Gaya, the place where Buddha sat under the famous Bodhi tree and became enlightened. Adiga juxtaposes Balram's elusive journey to enlightenment which seems like a paradoxically elusive goal in a post-modern setting. Adiga presents juxtaposing slices of Indian life which he befittingly divides into the zones of the 'dark' and the 'light'.

Balram's father is a poor rickshaw puller who dreams of a bright future for his son. Balram performs very well in school well but discontinues his education due to financial constraints. He gets his first break when he is picked as the driver for the landlord's son Ashok, and his American wife, Pinky. He thus graduates from a village-poor-boy to a smart driver earning a living by driving flashy cars in through uptown Delhi roads. Through the narrative, Adiga portrays the varied evils of the Indian social fabric which constitute issues such as - the elections, corruption, squalid conditions of the poor, oppressive 6 landlords, superstitions, familial responsibility, slavery and above all a slavish mindset. Adiga addresses the perspectives of a post-modern India through the narrative of Balram. Balram emerges as the White Tiger, a rare creature that appears once in a generation to undertake the metaphorical journey from the dark to the light. The novel presents the vision of the eternal journey of humanity from a sceptical post-modern lens.

Works Cited

Adiga, Aravind. The White Tiger. India: HarperCollins Publishers, 2008.

Nicol, Bran. The Cambridge Introduction to Postmodern Fiction. New York:

Cambridge University Press, 2009.

Sheoran, Jyoti and Pallavi. Postmodernism: Analysing Arvind Adiga's The White Tiger.

Shanlax. International Journal of English, Vol 6, 2018.

29.07.2021.http://www.shanlaxjournals.in/journals/ index.php/english/article/view/17

Sim, Stuart, ed. The Routledge Companion to Postmodernism. Cornwall: Routledge, 2001.

Singh, Sugandha. The White Tiger: A Post-Modern Reading. Web. Accessed 29.07.2021.

https://www.academia.edu/11034618/ THE_WHITE_TIGER_A_POSTMODERNIST_

Woods, Tim. Beginning Postmodernism. New York: Manchester University Press, 1999.

CHAPTER IV

PSYCHOPATH DON JUAN – A CULTURAL STUDY OF A MYSTERIOUS FIGURE IN BOTH LITERARY AND PRACTICAL CONTEXT

Dr. Gangadevi Sennimalai Marimuthu

Assistant Professor In English, Department of Foreign Languages

Faculty of Arts And Humanities, Albaha University, Kingdom of Saudi Arabia.

Introduction

Don Juan is considered as one of the Anti-Social behaviourism of all times in different cultures and societies. As a character in Literature once it was popular in western civilization. But now we can witness this fictitious character still existing in all cultural set-ups in the Indian community. As a result, this topic attracted many of the social activists, philosophers and even normal people of our society. The very name DON JUAN itself carries the meaning of the unchangeable character of a psychopath personality who builds relationships with his surroundings and environment in order to exploit and have control over whom he targets. An American Sociologist David G.Winter says that "To be sure, the terms Don Juanism and Don Juanesque are used in clinical practice to denote a type of man who practices (or who attempts) serial seduction" (Winter 1973, p. 168). This chapter discusses and highlights the psychological problem of the mentioned figure who transforms himself to be a serious seducer and betrayer in the society where he lives and how innocent women are affected by his traits. The level of perceptions varies from one culture to another based on their civilization.

• • •

Psychopath Don Juan – A Cultural Study of a Mysterious Figure in Both Literary and Practical Context

In earlier days there was a distinction between personal and private issues but now and then a large number of Females are facing the same trouble either in a private or public scenario. The characteristic features of the problem and its effects are the same since the beginning but the level of exposure is going beyond the control and getting mounted day by day. These Psychopaths never break their protocols and frame their own rules. High functioning Don Juan acts to be smarter and underestimates a woman whom he targets. But any Psychic man with the least functioning assumes and realizes that he will be exposed will soon disappear from the scene when the climax nears. A Don Juan normally develops a predator mentality with a positive hope to build trust for attracting meaningful gains by figuring out a perfect plan to set traps.

It is a little bit difficult to bring down such stereo-typed psychos since they never feel shame or have guilt about their actions. But the reality is to wait and watch, almost the majority of psychos are self-destructive and revealed to normal people for mechanizing and ends up being ostracized or driven away. Any kind of sympathy shown to these types of psychopaths suddenly infuriates them for no reason as they think that they are unique, smarter and self-made. A Psychopath believes that he is not affected by any neurological defects. But, the common observation about big Psychopaths is - one should be very careful while dealing with them as they are vengeful creatures who can harm and ruin your mental peace at any time. So, these type of Psychopathic Don Juan's who collapses the peace of an individual or group are in fact a bane to our existing society.

Don Juan – A negative cultural phenomenon in social consciousness

Don Juan is termed as a self-conscious and specific behaviour of wanting an erotic relationship. The very subject matter of this figure is bifurcated and expounded in a cultural context. On the other hand, he is known as a gallant partner, adoring philanderer, prodigy child of troubled pleasure and a womanizer and also we can justify by the very word DON JUAN as a man who is highly skilled and related to the art of seducing and loving. A Don Juan's Problem is a serious mental disorder that arose from a rooted deficiency syndrome. He is very significant sociologically because of his being feeble-minded with full of emotional derangement. As he faces serious emotional difficulty involving the issue of psychosis and neurosis disorders he cannot adjust to a socio-cultural environment. In a wider sense, we can see this theme as a social or cultural context where DON JUAN is termed as an IRRITATOR of the social morals.

Of course, every society needs this type of irritator in order to socialize and expose these diabolic demons in front of the public to create an awareness in the society where they live. As a result, they put their entire efforts to focus on this social evil to get rid of the same by identifying the majority of the personalities with the same disorder. Don Juan's 'colleague' Valmont, the sophisticated seducer of Choderlos de Lenclos's novel Les Liaisons dangereuses, puts it this way: My plan is to have her feel thoroughly the value and extent of each of the sacrifices she is going to make for me; not to lead her on so quickly that remorse cannot follow her; to make her virtue expire in slow agony; to fix her attention unceasingly on that distressing spectacle, and to grant her the happiness of having me in her arms only after she has been forced to admit this desire freely. (Letter LXX). Either earlier or later Don Juan's are not at all refined, yet women are fooled by his sugar-coated vows of extreme love and instant marriage concept, become victims of seductions.

Characteristics of a Don Juan

- Opportunists
- The diabolic flavour of Mockery
- finds seduction as a new trick
- affected by insecurities
- lack of self-confidence and self-esteem
- intolerant to frustrations
- unstable mind
- masked under depression
- lack of emotional attachment
- reasonless anxiety
- feeling isolated in spite of being with family members
- adopting a compulsive system
- self-exhaustion

Can a Psychopath Don Juan Ruin a Person's life?

Yes, of course, he can ruin anyone's life when his psyche functions hyper-active. No matter how proficient, efficient and humorous, he remains a sadist psychopath in seducing and ruining a woman's life. These ways are adopted to manipulate the innocents at an earlier stage for their self-upliftment. So if he is a given chance to take things for granted, he dares to play rotten games unless the very damage backfires. Originally these personalities with neurosis disorder are big scammers who can go to any extreme to spoil the name and fame and dare to ruin the life of a reputed innocent soul when he is stopped from taking advantage. Though the involved woman has adequate knowledge about his psychic behaviour and out of courtesy and humanity she may tolerate things initially but only to some extent later it never works out and literally, it leads him to adopt other ways to revenge her. Basically, a psychopath is not a power seeker or vengeful, he feels very secure and not intended to have control over the other, he remains practical for the sake of gaining favours (for example: for financial reasons, physical relationships and moral support outside his family). He is a buildup of super egoist stuff by nature. His primary intention is to derive benefits. A small psychopath keeps these strategies to maximize potential benefits and minimize the situation of getting endangered and being caught. He practices a cool and calm temperament to mask his attitude. He is not at all motivated by anything except being provoked by his ego consequently.

Don Juan – Domination over the woman whom he violates

From the traditional literary point of view, a Don Juan's problem is impossible to get rid of. Specifically, if his character is taken for debate, it clearly proves that it is interwoven with a well-established and prejudiced manner. Many philosophers have depicted their ideas on the archetypical seducers.The scholars' observations include the quotes of the final paragraph of Winter's chapter Don Juan - Don Juan lives out the secret ideal of many men, and hasa Power in a form of conquest; arising from an ambivalent fear of a powerful and binding mother, and symbolized by the sexual degradation of women. "Power is everything; yet it is nothing, for man can never escape *the encircling arms* [of death]" (Winter 1973, p. 200).

The very nature of his behaviorism is his cut-throat intention behind his attitude to maintain a tricky emotional bond with a woman to seduce her. These types of anti-humans are totally different from his society and friends circle. He is capable of tricking many and still finds as many as possible ways to trap women in his society. We can see many examples of heart-breaking incidents, but the recent one which shocked the entire nation is the talk of the town that happened in the state of Tamilnadu (Coimbatore district). The bitter truth is it happened in an educational institution that is hardly digestible. Here we can witness a Don Juan (Mithun Chakravarthy, a physics teacher of a private school who seduced an innocent 11th-grade female student that provoked her to extreme mental distress that lead to committing suicide) in the name of a teacher.

He never bothers about his social status and self-esteem in public since he knew that he can in any way dominate a woman with his fake emotional attachment and also very well known that no affected woman will go against him to make a complaint who will then lose the female identity and honour. They not only lose respect and dignity themselves alone but the reputation of their family and surroundings too. In his dictionary, if a woman is trying to expose his masked face means that is only a shame to that woman alone. Though he is not a rapist but considered a slow poisoner who expertise himself in mindreading to provoke the mind of a woman to exploit her with her own concern in the name of fake love and care. So according to law, he is the only responsible person for the damage that he caused to the victim whom he seduced and the punishment is declared only to the seducer.

Conclusion

Though Don Juan is not connected to rape, he is the only responsible person for the act he commits. A woman is not considered an equal partner in this crime. So either punishing or blaming her doesn't mean anything. The truth and reality are she is pre-planned and cheated in the name of emotional attachment. As a result, many women end up with everlasting distress, inflicted with pain and finally not able to overcome it and choose (death) the way of committing suicide to end up their life. The sole reason behind her decision is that she couldn't digest that she is being used and betrayed. A Don Juan ever hides his real identity with a strong woman to please her initially under a reputed mask but finally, he is weakened and exposed. He is seen as a person full of practical and bookish knowledge only to attract people to maintain relationships to show up and become popular among his surroundings. Logically it seems that he projects his masked character to create his own discourse to communicate and develop a relationship with a noble soul. In fact, his character is viewed as a person who is incapable of realizing a real emotional attachment. His transformation will be further a Psychopath initially, Sociopath gradually and a serial seducer finally. In simple terms, this type of womanizer who enjoys supremacy and mastery over a woman by tricky gestures will never be changed unless the law and society trap him under severe punishments.

Works Cited

FOUCAULT, M., 2001. The Subject and Power. In: Ed. James D. FAUBION. Trans.

ROBERT HURLEY et al. Power. Essential works of Foucault, 1954–1984. Vol. 3. London: Penguin.

SMEED, J. W., 1990. Don Juan: Variations On a Theme. London: Routledge.

WEINSTEIN, L., 1959. The Metamorphoses of Don Juan. Stanford: Stanford University Press.

WINTER, D. G., 1973. Don Juan: an archetype of the power motive. In: The Power Motive. Free Press.

https://psycnet.apa.org/record/2014-14524-021

https://www.tandfonline.com/doi/abs/10.1080/10611967.2020.1780836

Bio-Note

Dr. Gangadevi Sennimalai Marimuthu is currently working as an Assistant Professor of English, Department of foreign languages, Faculty of Arts and Humanities in Albaha University, Kingdom of Saudi Arabia. She has acquired her Bachelor's and Doctor of Philosophy in English Literature from Bharathiar University, Coimbatore; Post-Graduation and Master of Philosophy in English literature from M.K. University, Madurai and A Bachelor of Education Degree in English from Bharathidasan University, Trichy.

Her specialization in Ph.D. is Poetry in American literature and has published various research articles, poems and poetic drama in both English and Tamil languages. Apart from Presenting papers at National and International Conferences. She is an Athlete, a Volleyball player at the university level, a Motivational Speaker, fond of writing poems, short stories and essays on social issues and injustices against women and Society in both Tamil and

English languages. She is an optimist who firmly believes in fighting back tough situations and survives with positive hope. She has an infinite passion for music and a strong attitude towards independent thinking and acting within the limitations of Culture and Tradition. She is a Foreign Supervisor evaluating Ph.D. thesis for Bharathiar, Madurai Kamarajar, Annamalai, Thiruvalluvar, Manonmanium Sundaranar, Madras, Amrita Vishwa Vidyapeetham - Universities and the Central University of Punjab and so far 35 scholars are reported highly recommended and awarded Doctoral Degree. Academically she is dealing with Bachelor's, Masters and PhD programs with great enthusiasm and Professional Ethics creating interest among the Saudi Students.

• • •

CHAPTER V

PHONETICS: AN OVERVIEW

Dr. Alok Kumar Singh
Assistant Professor, Hindi Department
Maa Mansha Devi Mahavidyalaya, Chandauli

ABSTRACT

Words, syntax or sentences cannot be imagined without sound. The importance of sounds in any language cannot be denied. The set of sounds are words, phrases, sentences even language. In ancient Indian thought tradition also, the study of sounds has been done under Pratishakhya. Whereas in linguistics, the study of sounds is done under Phonetics. Phonology or phonetics is divided into three branches Articulatory Phonetics, Acoustic Phonetics, Auditory Phonetics on the basis of production, convection and reception of sounds. The study related to the pronunciation of sound is done under Articulatory phonetics. What is the place of pronunciation of sounds, which parts of speech are included in it, in what form does the air pronounce the sounds, that is, the study related to the production of sounds is done in this branch? Under Acoustic Phonetics, after the sound is pronounced, how the sound comes in contact with everyone through airwaves, that is, how these sounds reach between the speaker and the listener, is studied. The study related to the conduction of sounds is the basis of this branch.

Keyword: Phonetics, Phone, Phoneme, Allophone, Word, Syntax, Sentence, Morph and Morpheme

• • •

Sounds reach in our ears through airwaves in Auditory Phonetics. The study related to the hearing of sounds is done under Auditory Phonetics. How sounds enter through our ear and reach our brain through our nerve cells (neurons) and how the listener perceives the speech of the speaker through the image of substances and feelings located in the brain. All these are studied under this branch of phonetics, that is, the study related to the reception of sounds is the core of Auditory Phonetics.

The language is basically spoken. Words in spoken language are formed from sounds i.e. vocal sounds. People exchange their ideas through language. The sentence, Sub Sentence, Phrase, Word, Morpheme and Phoneme (sound) are respectively the smallest unit of language. The smallest unit in this is Phoneme (sound) i.e. the smallest unit of language is sound. The sentence, Sub Sentence, Phrase, Word and Morph or Morpheme etc. are all meaningful and all are formed from a group of sounds. Sounds are not meaningful in themselves, but they are meaningful. Sounds emanate from the human mouth. The lips, tongue, teeth, palate, alveolar, larynx, vocal cords, lungs, nasal cavity play an important role in the production of sounds. In this most of the work is done by the tongue. The most important element in the production of sounds is air. Sounds are classified on the basis of interruption, plosive, friction, the vibration of vocal cards etc. at any place in the mouth cavity of air. On the basis of how much air pressure is there, less or more, the vitality in consonant sounds is determined. If air comes out of the Nasal Cavity, then the sounds pronounced from it are called Nasal Sounds.

Language is a set of sounds emanating from the human mouth. Sounds are helpful in language formation. Sounds make words, the word makes the phrase, makes sub sentence, sub sentence makes sentences. A sentence is the biggest unit of language. Sound is called a phone from a linguistic point of view. The discipline under which sound is studied is called phonetics. The phone is the smallest unit of language. It is also known as sound. Without sound, language cannot even be imagined. In linguistics, the study context of the phone is called phonetics. Phonology has become an important branch in the serious study of linguistics. In English, the words Phonetics and Phonology are used for it, both of these words are formed from the Greek word Phone. Three aspects are reflected in the study of phone or sound producer, conductor, collector. The person or speaker who produces a phone or sound is called a voice producer. The collector or receiver is the listener, who receives the sound. The conducting medium is mainly in the form of airwaves.

The essentiality of the three parts in the phonetic process is self-evident. The existence of a phone (sound) is possible only when the sound will be produced by the cooperation of any two or more components of the different parts of the mouth. In the absence of the role of sound-producing components, the existence of sound is impossible. After the useful role of the sound-producing components, if there is a lack of a conductor or a convection medium, then it is impossible to feel the sound. Suppose a person makes a sound while sitting in an airtight chamber, then the airwave cannot come out of the chamber and the person outside cannot receive the sound. Thus the phonetics process gets blocked. In the absence of a third part collector or listener, the existence of sound production automatically becomes void. Thus, in the phonetics process, it is necessary to have all three speakers (producer), medium (conductor), the listener (collector).

There are two forms of sound, meaningful and meaningless. In linguistics, only meaningful sounds are studied. In the sound production process, air comes out from either the mouth or nose. Thus, sound can be divided into two categories, nasal and non-nasal sound. In the pronunciation of sounds, air comes out from the nostrils along with the mouth, it is called nasal sound. The sound in which the air comes out of the mouth only is called non-nasal or oral sound. On the basis of intensity and slowness of sound, it can be divided into three classes Naad, Breath and Japit. When the vocal cords are mixed with each other in the production of sound, then air comes out by pushing them, such sound is called naad sound, such as ग्, घ्, ज् etc. It is also called voiced sound. When the vocal cords are away from each other, the air of inhalation comes out easily without friction. Such a sound is called breathing or voiceless; like क्, त्, प् etc. When there is a very low sound, air comes out from any corner of both the vocal cords. Such sound is called the Japit sound.

Phonology has special importance in the study of linguistics because the knowledge of other larger units is based on it. The study of various sound-producing components is done under this only. After the right knowledge of phones, the right writing gets a strong basis. It is also possible to know the changes in different contexts that occur in pronunciation. Phonology is the study of various sounds along with the detailed analysis of the process of their production. In this study, the composition and role of different organs producing sound are also studied. The representation of sound quality and its significance is also done. Along with the phone, the analysis of Phoneme is also done. The form of the alphabet and its classification are also considered. Different sounds keep on changing according to time, situation and experiment. In the context of sound change, various scholars have prescribed some sound rules. Along with the study of these laws, the directions of sound change and the causes of sound change are considered.

Words like phonograms etc. are also used for phonemes. The word phoneme is much newer than phonogram, but nowadays its use is going on. There is no consensus among scholars regarding the nature of phonemes. Different scholars have considered it related to different subjects. Bloomfield and Daniel Jones have accepted it as a physical entity. Edward Sapir considers it a psychological entity. W. F. Twodle considers the phoneme as an abstract imaginary entity. Change of meaning does not always take place due to a change of phone or sound whereas the semantic change is definite from the phoneme change. A phoneme is the smallest unit of spoken language that distinguishes between two sounds. Thus it is also clear that phoneme is related to sound. If the sound is related to pronunciation, then it is also related to hearing. If the sound is not heard then its existence will also be doubtful. The phoneme is said to be related to physiology and physics because of the pronunciation of sound and the relationship of hearing because if the pronunciation and hearing process is related to physiology, then the convection process is completely related to physics.

The basic sounds of any language are about fifteen to fifty. On the determination of these sounds, the phoneme is determined. The difference between sounds is displayed through the phoneme itself. ज, न, प are different phonemes, hence there is a difference between them. The difference between जान and पान is based on the difference of phoneme. Here ज and प are two different meaningful sounds. On the basis of these different meaningful sounds, there is also a difference in meaning between जान and पान. These meaningful sounds are called phonemes in phonetics. There is a subtle difference between the न sounds of those two words because if a person pronounces the same sound twice, it is natural to have subtle differences in them such as पान, जान, पानी, मनु, मीनू, माने, मानो etc. There is normally no difference between the different न sounds, but on subtle contemplation, there is knowledge of subtle differences in these sounds. Phonetically, if there is a difference between them, then there is sufficient similarity between them on the basis of place of pronunciation, effort and reason, etc., the basis of the concept of the phoneme. To graph the phonemes, we use this type of basis by adopting क / म / ल of कमल.

A phoneme is the smallest unit of language such as अ, त, क, प etc. The phoneme represents different similar sounds. If a sound is uttered in more than one way or in many ways, then there will be only one phoneme for it, such as अ sound is spoken by ten people or if the same person is spoken ten times then it will have ten forms, but these ten sounds. There will be only one phoneme for the forms. A phoneme is a semantic unit that is the difference in meaning between the words, body and mind is due to the difference between the phonemes त and म. There is a subtle difference in the pronunciation of neither body nor mind, but both are related to the same phoneme, so there is no difference of meaning between them. The phoneme is related to the spoken language.

It has nothing to do with written language. A similar unit in the written language is writing. अ in Hindi is a phoneme for which many articles are used in English; For example, C > कैमल (camel), K > काइट (kite) > केमेस्ट्री (chemistry), Que >चैक (cheque), CK > बैक (back) etc. Each language has its own phonemes, which are different from the phonemes of any other language, that is, the phonemes are based on the particular language e.g. प, फ are the phonemes of Hindi, whereas in other languages these sounds can also be there. When a person uses the phonemes of another language other than the phonemes of his own language, there is difficulty in their pronunciation. At such time, it is not possible to identify different language-speakers on the basis of differences in phonemes, if there is जल in Hindi then जाल in Bengali. Phonemes are influenced by concordant sounds, when the sound of त Voiceless, Hypnosis, Dental sound is used with न, then the effect of the nasal sound न falls on it तन>ताँन.

There is a certain arrangement of sounds in all languages, on the basis of which phonetic balance is maintained in them like क, घ, छ, झ, ठ, ढ etc. of Hindi. If there is knowledge of phonemes, then according to the order of hypnosis, aspirate, according to the phoneme arrangement, in addition to घ in क class, the possibility of ख another aspirate sound will become clear. In this way, the phoneme arrangement is completed. Sometimes the two sounds are used interchangeably without changing the meaning. This usually occurs in the case of simplification of dialects, but sometimes such usages are found in standard pronunciation as क़ > क, ख़ > ख, ज़ > ज (इल्ज़ाम). The meaning of the first word is दोष and the meaning of the second is घोड़े के मुँह में लगाम देना here both the words are used in the same दोष meaning. Each language has a different number of phonemes. If a sound is once certain that it is phoneme, it will always be phonemic in every situation. If any sound is found in any one of the beginning, middle and end, then the phonemic status is worth considering. Such a situation is not seen in Hindi, English sounds become Ph, Th, Kh respectively in the initial position of p + k, but remain the same as P.T.K in the middle and the end. The sound introduced is only in the beginning, its meaning does not change either. Lastly, there is no phoneme. Due to being used in more surroundings in the middle and end positions p. t. k. are self-contained. These sounds are allophones among themselves.

With the knowledge of phonemes, there is ease in the correct pronunciation of the language. It is only through the phoneme that the basic sounds of a language are known. In this way, phoneme knowledge has special importance in language teaching. The phoneme is related to spoken language. Through this, the number of sounds of the language is controlled due to this type of control, a proper system is maintained in language pronunciation. It is easier and easier to learn new sounds when they come up with the phoneme system. A phoneme is a semantic unit of language. Knowledge of other units of language like Word, Syntax, and Sentence etc. is not possible unless there is knowledge of Phoneme, because the language itself is based on the later larger units Phoneme. Phoneme plays an important role in script formation. The script is formed only after the determination of the phonemes of a language.

In this way, Phonemes can be called the foundation of the script. The ideal script is decidedly through the phoneme. The script which has a script for a phoneme is called a model script. It is through Phoneme that the form of International Script (I.N.P.A) has emerged. There is a proper arrangement of one symbol for different phonemes of all languages. In this way, phoneme plays an important role in the correct pronunciation of the language, ideal script and international script formation etc.

Other branches of linguistics such as morphology, syntax and semantics are essentially based on sound. Sounds form forms, forms form words and sentences. The basis of such meaning is the word or sentence. Unless there is proper knowledge of sounds, it is difficult to have proper knowledge of morphology, syntax and semantics. Knowledge of sounds is also essential for the formation of script marks. There are languages spoken in the world even today which do not have any script of their own. The knowledge of sounds is essential for the formation of their scripts. The ideal script is considered to be one in which the arrangement of a script symbol for a sound is given. The Devanagari script would be said to be an ideal script, whereas the Roman script does not have this quality. For example, where there is a script for क in Hindi, while in Roman six k, c, q, ck, cc, ch similar to c, there is a sense of स and somewhere else of क somewhere च. Roman has five script marks (a, e, i, o, u) for vowels, making for twenty-one vowels in English. That is to say that proper knowledge of sounds is necessary for making script symbols. There were no ढ़ and ड़ sounds in Sanskrit but there are in Hindi. In Sanskrit, क्रीडति was the word पीडा which is how we pronounce it today as क्रीड़ति and पीड़ा. Today the Sanskrit words दृढ, गूढ, रूढ are pronounced as दढु, गढू and रूढ. From a linguistic point of view, the correct pronunciation of sounds is a sign of good language. One cannot have a good grasp of any language unless there is knowledge of correctly pronouncing the sounds of those languages. Therefore, if proper knowledge of the Hindi language is to be obtained, then correct pronunciation and alphabetical knowledge of Hindi sounds are necessary. With this, not only will Hindi be spoken well, but a good knowledge of the Hindi language will also be obtained.

Works Cited

1. Abercrombie, D. (1964) English phonetic texts. Faber.
2. Abercrombie, D. (1965) Studies in phonetics and linguistics. Oxford U.P.
3. Ball, M. J. (1997) Instrumental clinical phonetics. London: Whurr Publishers.
4. Carlos Gussenhoven (2004) The phonology of tone and intonation. Cambridge: Cambridge University Press.
5. Carr, Philip, 1953- (2013) English phonetics and phonology: an introduction. 2nd ed. Chichester, UK: Wiley-Blackwell.
6. Daniel Jones (1972) An outline of English phonetics. 9th ed. Cambridge: Heffer.
7. Harrington, J. (2010) Phonetic analysis of speech corpora. Oxford: Wiley-Blackwell.
8. Jacques Durand and Bernard Laks (2002) Phonetics, phonology and cognition. Oxford: Oxford University Press.
9. Katamba, F. (1989) An introduction to phonology. London: Longman.

10. Katrina Hayward (2000) Experimental phonetics. London: Longman.
11. Ladefoged, P. (1996) Elements of acoustic phonetics. 2nd ed. Chicago, Ill: University of Chicago Press.
12. Malmberg, B. (1963) Phonetics. New York, N.Y.: Dover Publications.
13. Noel Burton-Roberts (ed.) (2000) Phonological knowledge: conceptual and empirical issues. Oxford: Oxford University Press.

CHAPTER VI

INFLUENCE OF SOCIAL MEDIA IN WOMEN IN KERALA

Dr. Geetha Lakshmi

Guest Faculty, Bishop Abraham Memorial College Mallappally, Thuruthicadu, Pathanamthitta, Kerala.

ABSTRACT

Ever since human existence there exist certain communication between them which makes human beings unique as compared to other living organisms. From very early times there exist power, discrimination, and inequality within the human society that is based on gender- male and female. Modern civilized societies are giving equal status to men and women through various legislative measures in this matter. Even after all these efforts still, our society is not free from such maladies. The influence of media on the subject nowadays is increasing because of the recent development in the field of information technology. Information is at the fingertips throughout the world with the rapid developments in the field of computer science. Women empowerment means creating self strength and efficiency building in women in the social, economic, political and psychological fields.

The government has come up with various schemes such as Beti Bachao, Beti Padhao Yojana, Mahila E Haat Yojana, Mahila Shakti Kendra, Working Women Hostel, Sukanya Samriddhi Yojana etc, to empower women. This investigation is to arrive at the present scenario of all the above-specified facts- Media and Women Empowerment-positive and negative effects in detail.

Keywords: Cyberbullying and Empowerment.

• • •

Introduction

Media can be defined as the technologies that are intended to reach a large audience through mass communication. Social media has changed our lives in positive and negative ways.

Social media helps to maintain friendships and other positive relationships. The use of platforms like Watsapp, Facebook, Instagram and, Twitter are helping to create a strong relationship between family members, friends and relatives. With social media, people can share pictures and videos and communicate with their close ones. This has strengthened relationships compared to the past.

Social media made it easy for job seekers to get access to job posts according to their tastes. And in different sites in social media helpful to build different skills, and to know about unknown things.

Businesses have been greatly impacted by social media from marketing to interacting with customers on a timely basis. And also advertising through social media is pretty cost-friendly as compared to costs incurred by print, TV or other traditional media. After purchase, the goods their interaction and feedback to the customers is helpful to understand the taste and preference of the customers and to find any need for the adoption of new strategies.

Different studies are conducted in this area and one of the studies reveals that the major percentage of the social media user population is the younger generation, teenagers and middle-aged people[1]. Social media is easily accessible. Social media opens the potential for direct access to clients without any third-party intervention.

Social media attracted a *massive* number of users with an estimate of 3.5 billion users worldwide.

Irrespective of whether the interaction is voluntary or involuntary, it has also negative sides. Searching online there is some form of internet security that should protect you from hackers, thief's, identity theft and viruses, they live many miles away.

The negative impact of social media is on society has created some generation barriers. An elderly person would generally not understand the value of life for their children. Kids are very fond of using different social gadgets, they think these are the true source of enjoyment and pleasure. They always keep an eye on what in the market is new. As a result, a lack of studies among them is being seen which itself is unfortunate. This is no doubt, that it is also a failure of our parents and teachers who can't divert their attention to the rapid use of social media.

This is one of the serious problems faced by our community with the use of internet media. Women harassment has been increased because of the influence of social media. Teenagers see different dramas and movies based on the harassment of women. The way media portray women and men in these dramas makes the audience feel extremely comfortable with the kidnapping, teasing, and disrespecting the women (physically or morally). So, they try to implement the same in their life.

The new generation who see different sorts of dramas, movies, and plays, are now more interested in new friendships. They do not bother whether the person is elder to him, they just try to have the same circumstances as they normally see in social media. Children get in superiority and sometimes inferiority complex by the frequent use of social media.

The cases of street crimes, robberies and kidnapping have been increased due to social media. The new generation sees people doing the crime with complete liberty in dramas and no one is after them. They think that they will plan the perfect crimes. So, they apply the same for them. It also causes shame and trouble for their family members.

As teens see their friends having a luxurious life, they try to have the same in their life. They ask for money from their parents. Sometimes, they steal in their home items, if their demand for money is unfulfilled. In this situation, kids cross their limits and start stealing. They forget the difference between right and wrong and prefer to satisfy their need.

Online social platforms are *addictive* and this has drastically reduced the learning skills of the students, social relations believe, family unity, productivity at workplaces etc., Cyberbullying [3] is another worrying impact of social media. Because information travels faster online but, a piece of false information could quickly reach a big number of people and cause great panic among the recipients.

The objective of the study

1. To find out the impact of social media on the social life of women in Kerala
2. To find out the positive and negative effects of social media.
3. To explore how social media turned against women.
4. To find suggestions and recommendations for policy options.

Methodology

In this study, both primary and secondary data were used. Primary data were collected from different age groups of women 6-14, 15-59 and above 60, both rural and urban populations through interview method. The area for the selection of the study is Ezumattoor panchayath and Tiruvalla Municipality in Pathanamthitta District. The size of the sample was selected by 66 females from rural areas and 334 from urban areas.

Sampling design

Considering the selection of women, stratified random sampling is adopted to take 400 females on a stratified random basis from among a total of 33598 females in both rural and urban areas. From 334 females are selected out of 28066, from Tiruvalla Municipality, 66 females are selected out of 5532 from Ezumattoor Panchayath. The equi-proportionate method with Slovin's formula *N1+N(0.05)2* was used to select 400 females from both the rural and urban areas.

Universe of study

The area for the selection of the study is Ezumattoor panchayath and Tiruvalla Municipality in Pathanamthitta District.

Table 1: Population characteristics of study area

	Male	Female	Total
Tiruvalla	24,817	28,066	52,883
Ezumattoor	5166	5532	10698

Source: Census 2011

The subject, the Influence of social media can empower women is of great importance in Kerala. Where there is 100 percentage literacy and more than 50 % of the population consist of women. Women empowerment means creating self strength and efficiency building in women in the social, economic, political and psychological fields. Empowerment literally means giving power or authority women should be given equal opportunity in every field irrespective of any gender discrimination. Respecting women, starting giving equal opportunities, encouraging them to take up jobs, giving higher education, taking up business activities etc, are the modern concerns of our Government.

Conclusion

Social media is a powerful revolution that has changed our lives to a great extent. It has changed our social relations, education, businesses, political affairs, professions and job opportunities, therefore this study gives insights into the areas that have been significantly affected in our society especially women.

Our social set-up is based on gender ie, men are supposed to be the earning members and the family decision making is vested upon them. Women are supposed to do the household work and are involved in the upbringing of the children. Women are subject to heinous crimes like - rape, acid attack, dowry system and domestic violence- all are the evils of our society even now.

No doubt, media really has a role in empowering women especially when every Kerala woman almost owns an android mobile phone. With the use of such devices, social networking changed the way people interact with each other. Social networking has changed the general outlook of our lives with Email. Messaging through sharing of stories, photos, communication with others involves the use of different applications like WhatsApp, Facebook, Instagram, youtube etc. The positive side of it is that we can have contact with friends, meet new people, provide educational benefits as well as the convenience of mobility access. The negative side of it include identity theft, cyberbullying, decreased social interaction in real life and social isolation.

Works Cited

1. Babu, Jobi, and P. Jayakumar. "Attitude and Awareness of Women about Cyber Sexual Offences: An Area of Social Work Intervention." *Studies in Indian Place Names* 40.72 (2020): 204-216.
2. Charles, Drupa Dinnie, et al. "Performing gender, doing politics: social media and women election workers in Kerala and Tamil Nadu." *Proceedings of the 2020 International Conference on Information and Communication Technologies and Development*. 2020.

3. Devika, J., and Mini Sukumar. "Making space for feminist social critique in contemporary Kerala." *Economic and Political Weekly* (2006): 4469-4475.
4. Kapoor, Shraddha. "Women in Kerala: A Commentary." *Making of Distinctions: Towards a Social Science of Inclusive Oppositions* (2021): 223.
5. PRIYADARSHINI S, How women-only communities on social media helped women cope with the stress of the lockdown, The Hindu, June 19, 2020.
6. The report, Importance and Benefits of Social Media in Today's World, inspirationfeed.com, January 2, 2020.
7. Saji, Joyal Alias, Bichu P. Babu, and Shaliet Rose Sebastian. "Social influence of COVID-19: An observational study on the social impact of post-COVID-19 lockdown on everyday life in Kerala from a community perspective." *Journal of Education and Health Promotion* 9 (2020).
8. Sheela, K. D. "Effectiveness Of Social Media On Youth In Relation To Their Social Life In Kerala." *Turkish Journal of Computer and Mathematics Education (TURCOMAT)* 12.6 (2021): 923-933.
9. Social Media Statistics, 2019.
10. Vinson Kurian, In connected Kerala, social media can sway results in half the seats: report, The Hindu, January 20, 2018.

[1]Importance and Benefits of Social Media in Today's World, inspirationfeed.com, January 2, 2020.

[2] According to 2019 Social Media Statistics.

[3] Results of cyberbullying have seen victims falling into depression and, in more radical cases, has cost them their lives.

CHAPTER VII

ROLE OF ENGLISH LANGUAGE DURING PRE-INDEPENDENCE AND POST-INDEPENDENCE INDIA: A CRITICAL APPRAISAL

Dinesh Kumar

Assistant Professor in English

Dyal Singh College, Karnal

ABSTRACT

There is no doubt in denying the fact that before the independence of India to the present time, one can witness numerous changes in the evolution of the English language in India. Facing a number of ups and downs, the English language has now become an important and vital part of social, cultural, political and academic fields with its prime importance as a language of opportunity. Gaining fluency and competence in the English language is a passport to one's bright future, and the lack of it is a big drawback for anyone at present. Moreover, thinking of the progress and prosperity of a nation like India is like a daydream in the absence of the growth of English. A nation will never be able to progress and flourish if it is not paying attention to including English in its curriculum of it.

Keywords: Language, foreign, lingua-franca, privileged, history, unite.

• • •

Role of English Language During Pre-Independence and Post-Independence India: A Critical Appraisal

Language is a means through which a child contemplates the past, grapes the present, and approaches the future. It goes without saying that language plays an important role in the mental, emotional and social development of a person. Though English is a foreign language, it occupies a unique place in India. Whether we are at home, in the state, or out of the state, in the country, or away from, English is important and it continues to hold a unique position. The English language has been playing a significant and vital role in shaping the ideas of people. Regarding its importance, Pandit Jawaharlal Nehru has rightly said that "The English language is our's historic necessity". English has been important, is important, and will continue to remain an important language in India. It is taught and learnt with affection and love and, that is why it enjoys a privileged position in our country. English is not only a national language of England, but it is also an international language. It may be called the language of world civilization as none should underestimate the importance of English. Even M.K. Gandhi also asserted in this direction: "I hold its knowledge as a second language to be indispensable for specified Indian who have to represent the country's interest in the international domain. I regard the English language as an open window for peeping into Western thought and science".

English has its unique importance in our country as it has played a very vital and significant role in building modern India. It has become one of the major languages of the world, and Indians can neglect its study at their own risk. Its richness, its flexibility, its elegance, its dignity seem to behave seem to have made it universally popular as we also find in the words of Nehru when he says: "one hundred and fifty years of personal contact has made English an integral part of our educational system and this cannot be changed without injury to the cause of education in India".

English has been regarded as a link language that, no doubt, joins together different states of India. People living in different states of India can communicate in English besides their own native language. People living in different states speak their own regional language, but the leaders from different states meet sometimes on the common platform. By using this language, they can convey their thoughts to one another. The language link is a greater link between us and the English speaking people than any political link for the commonwealth link, or anything else. It is so because we can see how their thoughts are functioning much more than the other European languages. Thus, we find that the use of English has been a unifying factor.

As far as English in India is concerned, it has contributed a lot in imparting educational importance. It has been the medium of instruction in schools and colleges. Even today, a large number of people send their children to English medium schools. Higher education in Science, medicine, engineering and technology is not possible without English. Most of the good books on all these subjects are available in the English language only.

Apart from it, English also plays a dominant role is trade and industry as we find that big businessmen use English in their correspondence. National and international trade takes place in English as they use English in the maintenance of their accounts and in giving instructions. Without English, success in the commercial area is not at all possible.

Keeping all these factors in our mind, we can find out that English is enjoying international importance as it is used on international levels. Being used all over the world, it has attained international importance. It links together people of different nations of the world. Through English, we can develop political, cultural and economic relations with the rest of the world. So, the English language is indispensable for us as Mahatma Gandhi has rightly observed in this context when he says: "English is a language of international commerce; it is also the language of diplomacy and it contains many rich literary treasures; it gives us an introduction to the Western thoughts and culture."

The English language helps in international trade and industry which leads to better understanding between the different nations of the world. The latest and updated information in all the fields of science and technology is available only in the English language. A person knowing English finds opportunities for employment almost in every country. It also helps in bringing people of different nations close and intimate to each other. In addition to it, English has also cultural importance which helps in bringing people of different cultures closer to each other. It also assists in our inter-cultural understanding inside the country. It is through the medium of English that we are able to keep the different cultural groups of India united. In fact, English has helped us in building new cultural traditions. It has also resulted in the process of modernisation of Indian society.

The study of English culture has taken out ignorance and superstitions from the mind of the Indian people. It has brought a wealth of knowledge and experience to India. From the cultural point of view, English has great importance. It is, undoubtedly, a language of modern scientific culture.

English has been serving as a window on the world and the study of English by Indians serves the purpose of a window. Through this window, we can peep into what is happening all around us. In the same way, the study of English helps us to know the progress being made by the people of different nations of the world in different areas of life. F.G. French rightly observes in this direction when he asserts: “a traveller who can speak English will find somebody who can understand him wherever he may go; anyone who can read English can keep in touch with the whole world without leaving his own house”.

English informs us about the advancement taking place throughout the world. It may be the field of science, technology, machine or it may be any human creativity, we come to know about it through this language. It mirrors to us everything in the true sense of words. Our country cannot afford to close the window of the English language. English is also playing an equally significant and vital role in our social life. People cannot progress without the language of English in their life as the majority of educated people use this language for correspondence. They find it more convenient to converse in English. It is the means of social and intellectual communication in the highly educated sections of society. In marriages and parties, mostly the invitation cards are printed in the English language. In our daily conversation, we use a large number of English words. It has become very useful in our social life.

At the administrative level also, English is playing a dominant role as we find that English has been the official language in our country for more than one hundred and fifty years. Even now, it has almost the same position as in the offices of the country. No doubt, some states have made strong efforts for developing their own regional language, but have not been able to replace English. Almost at every level of administration, we find that English alone is being used in the District Courts, High Courts, and Supreme Courts, cases are prepared and presented in English. Thus, we find that English dominates in our country at different levels of administration.

English is also serving as a foreign language which is already known to the Indians. In this age of globalisation and competition, everyone wants to excel the others. Some people are interested in learning more languages, and the need to learn some foreign languages is also there. Now the question arises which foreign language should be learnt? English is a language already popular with the Indians. We have people who can teach this language. We also have English literature produced by Indian poets, novelists and dramatists. So, it would be better if we learn this language. We have a suitable climate already created in our country for the development and growth of the English language.

The knowledge of English also serves as a passport for the employment of the Indian people. The knowledge of English provides a privileged position to a person. People with good knowledge of English are given preference for selections. After the departure of English from our country, its position underwent a tremendous change. It became an important study to know the position of this language during the English period in our country and after the English rule.

During the Pre-Independence period, English enjoyed the privileged position as the queen language. During the British rule in India, English enjoyed the topmost position because it was the first language in the whole country. It was the lingua-franca of the literature. In every walk of life, it was the vehicle of thought and activity. The importance given to it was not envy of everyone, and in no way, it creates any jealousy. It was the pride of all. English is serving as a medium of instruction at different levels. English used to be the medium of instruction at school and college levels in some of the elementary schools. Also, English was used as a medium of instruction as everybody loved to study different subjects through this language. The study of English was meant for all the children who join the school. Our elders speak English very nicely the main reason being behind it is that they were taught mostly in English. All subjects, whether English, history or Geography, was generally taught by the Englishmen, and the students were under the impact of the Englishmen for a good deal of time.

They learnt to speak English of the native speakers. That is why, our elderly person, whose schooling career belongs to that era, can speak a class English. English is introduced right from the beginning of the schooling of the children. Everybody was proud of it because the schooling of this language was considered a passport for employment. We find English was of great importance before the freedom of our country, but with the passage of time, there have been a number of changes in the position of English in our country. After the independence in 1947, India became free and English people left India for good. The whole administration, the language policy, came into the hands of the Indian authorities. the very question regarding the place of English in India became controversial. Some leaders argued that English should be uprooted from the country, whereas some other favoured the retention of English.

Mahatma Gandhi said in this regard: “it is my considered opinion that English education, in the matter it was it has become given, has emasculated the English educated Indians. It has put a severe strain upon the Indian students and made us imitators". He, further, said, "all the superstitions that India has, none is so great as that a knowledge of the English language is necessary for imbibing ideals of liberty and developing accuracy of thought". But, another person like C. Rajagopalachari says that English should be retained in our country. His considered opinion was- "we in our anger and the hatred against the British people should not throw away the baby (English) with the English people.

Maulana Abul Kalam, soon after taking over the education portfolio in the Indian government, said at a press conference: "so far as general studies are concerned, it was never my intention to suggest that there should be any falling in the standard of English". In the words of a Pandit Jawaharlal Nehru, "one hundred years and fifty years of intimate contact have made English an integral part of our educational system, and this cannot be changed without injury to the cause of education in India.

In addition to it, English has today become one of the major languages of the world and Indians can neglect the study of English at their own risk of loss to themselves. Indian considered that in the future as well as the standard of the teaching English should be maintained as high as possible".

In fact, for the first two or three years of Independence, so much was said but nothing concrete could be decided. In 1950, when the Indian constitution was framed, it was unanimously decided to continue English as the official language of the country for fifteen years. During this period, all efforts were made to develop Hindi-the national language of the country. The Indian authorities thus hoped to replace English with Hindi in due course of time, but there was great opposition by the people living in the Southern part of the country.

The result was that in 1963, the parliament passed a bill according to which English was to be declared as an associate official language of India for an indefinite period. In 1968, the National Policy on education adopted by the government of India focused on English as the need of the hour. With the passage of time, some of the states adopted their regional languages as the official language, but they could not make the Hindi language the link between the different states of free India. So, in order to continue the link between the various state of India, English continued to be a unifying factor.

Works Cited

1. Catford, J.C. *A Linguistic Theory of Translation.* London: Oxford University Press, 1969.
2. Donough, J. *ESP: Teaching the Teachers, Language Training.*London: Oxford University Press,1988.
3. Dudley-Evans T & St. Jhons MJ. *Developments in English for Specific Purposes.* New York: Cambridge University, 1998.
4. Hedge T. *Teaching and Learning in the Language Classroom.* London: OUP Oxford, 2000.
5. Hutchinson T. & Waters A. *English for Specific Purpose: A Learning Centred Approach.* New York: Cambridge University Press, 1987.
6. Jordan R.R. *English for Academic Purposes: A Guide and Resource Book for Teachers.* New York: Cambridge University Press, 1997.
7. Kachru B, Kachru Y & Nelson C. *The Handbook of World English.*New Delhi: Blackwell Publishing, 2006.

8. Lewis M. *Implementing the Lexical Approach, Language Teaching. Publication*. London: Oxford Press, 1997.
9. Lightbown PM & Spada N. *How Languages are Learned.* New York: Oxford University Press 1993.
10. Bansal, R.K. & Harrison, J.B. *Spoken English.* Madras: Orient Longman, 1994.
11. Scrivener, J. *Learning Teaching.* New Delhi: Macmillian Education, 2011.
12. Slade, D. Conversation: *From Description to Pedagogy.* CUP, 2005.
13. Verma, S.K. & Krishnaswamy N. *Modern Linguistics: An Introduction.* Delhi: Oxford University Press, 1989.
14. Widdowson, H. *Learning Purpose and Language Use.* England: Oxford, 1983.

CHAPTER VIII

GENERAL INDIAN ENGLISH: A WAY FORWARD

Mr. Bhaskara Rao Chintha

Assistant Professor, Department of Science and Humanities,

St.Martin's Engineering College, Dhulapally, Secunderabad, Telangana.

ABSTRACT

This article is about resolute investigate the differences of pronunciations between British English and Indian English. Many Indians claim that their English is analogous to land English; actually, they're different within the level of pronunciation of certain words. The quality of pronunciation aimed is predicated on accepted Indian usage modified within the direction of British Received Pronunciation to realize International intelligibility. English, as spoken by educated people in India, doesn't differ radically from native English in grammar and vocabulary, but in pronunciation, it's different from both British and Indian English languages. Even within India, there are an outsized number of regional varieties, each different from the opposite in certain ways, and retaining to some extent the phonetic patterns of the Indian Language spoken therein particular region. These regional forms of English are sometimes not even mutually intelligible. In many regions, however, there are folks that have shaken off the gross features of regional accent and speak a more 'neutral' style of Indian English.

Keywords: Received Pronunciation (RP), General Indian English (GIE), Intelligibility and Lingua-franca

Introduction:

In this paper, I've got tried to figure on the English pronunciation of Indian Natives and also how it differs from British Received Pronunciation. The quality of pronunciation aimed relies on accepted Indian usage modified within the direction of British Received pronunciation to achieve International intelligibility. In spite of the adaptation of Hindi as the official language of the Union of India, it is officially English that continues to function as the language of the government of India. The most official correspondence is still carried on in India, English. English is still the 'lingua franca' for educational people from different parts of India who do not share a common Indian language, and it is also the only foreign language by a large number of people. It has been gaining greater importance for global communication. It is no longer just a 'library language' but a language of opportunities. "English is a guest language- the language on which the sun doesn't set and where sunset never sleeps," says Randolf Gerrik.

Overview:

India with about twenty-three million speakers of English is the third largest English speaking nation after the U.S.A. and U.K. English has been playing a vital role in the educational system as well as in the national life in India. In India English is the language of banking, commerce and industry. It is the medium of instruction in higher education like medicine, engineering, science and technology. It is the Associate Official language for interstates and the centre. English is necessary for national opportunities in education, employment and business at a higher level. There are, indeed, several varieties of English spoken in India, each variety being strongly coloured by the mother tongue of the speakers of these varieties of English.

A brief history of Indian English:

Indian English is that a group of English dialects, or regional language varieties, spoken totally on the Indian subcontinent. English language public instruction began in India within the 1830s during the rule of the Malay Archipelago Company. In 1837, English replaced Persian because of the official language of the corporate. At the time of India's independence in 1947, English was the sole functional inter-language within the country. Consequently, although the Constitution of India (1951) declared Hindi the official language of the new republic, it retained English because of the associate official language. After Indian Independence in 1947, Hindi was declared the primary official language and wanted to make Hindi an only national language in parliament, but it did not happen. Moreover, English is now reckoned as the most indispensable. As an example, it's the sole reliable means of day-to-day communication between the central government and also non- Hindi states. The spread of a people language in India has led it to become adapted to suit the local dialect.

In general, Indian English is meant a certain variety of English spoken by educated Indians. General Indian English is free from regional features. Indian English as spoken by educated people in India does not differ radically from native English in grammar and vocabulary. It is in pronunciation that Indian English is different from either British or American English. The most important Pan-Indian feature is that /**p**/, /**t**/, /**k**/ are generally un-aspirated in all positions. Most of the Indian the retroflex plosives /ṭ /, / ḍ/ in the place of the alveolar plosives / t/ and /**d**/ which occur in English. Many Indians use the voiced labio-dental frictionless continuant / **ʋ** / in place of both /**v**/ and /**w**/ which occurs in English.

The Vowel System of General Indian English:

As opposed to the 12 vowel system of Received Pronunciation (RP), General Indian English (GIE) has a vowel system consisting of eleven pure vowels and six diphthongs. These vowels make difference in pronunciation. Some of them are discussed here

Difference between General Indian English and Received Pronunciation

- The English spoken in Great Britain is regarded as the original and authentic English. Oxford University has standardized the English language and authenticated the dialect used at Oxford. The IPA or International Phonetic Alphabet has created the Received Pronunciation or R.P of British English or B.E accordingly.
- Owing to the Sanskrit root of most Indian languages, the Indian tongue is more accustomed to pronouncing English words in a different manner.
- General Indian English distinctly pronounces the consonant / **r** / following a vowel whereas in R.P it remains silent.
- General Indian English does not distinguish in pronunciation of the different forms of / **a** /. It stresses on a long / **a:** / for every pronunciation thus the words ‘far’ and ‘fur’, ‘message’ and ‘massage’ are pronounced in the same way.

- There is no R.P for '**o**' in British English, so the words 'go', 'so' are pronounced with a diphthong. But in General Indian English they are pronounced with the sound '**o**'.
- General Indian English does not pronounce '**u**' as / **iu** / so the word 'student' is not pronounced as / st**ju**:dnt / but as / st**u**:dent /.

The Vowel system of general Indian English:

Word	RP	Indian English
Low	/ləʊ/	/lo:/
don't	/ dəʊt /	/do:nt/
Holes	/ həʊlz/	/ ho:lz/

Indians tend to use / **o:** / in the place of / **əʊ** / a diphthong in RP

Word	RP	Indian English
Main	/ meɪn /	/me:n/
Train	/ treɪn /	/ tre:n /
Play	/ pleɪ/	/ ple: /

- Indians make RP diphthong /**e** ɪ / as monophthong / e: /

Word	RP	Indian English
Poor	/ pʊə /	/ pu:/
Tour	/ tʊə /	/ tu:/
Sour	/ sʊə /	/ su:/

- Indians tend to use / u:/ in the place of / ʊə / a diphthong in RP

Word	RP	Indian English
Parents	/ peərənts /	/ pe:rents /
Area	/ eəriə /	/ e:riə /
Fair	/ feə /	/ fe: /

- Indians use / **e:** / in the place of / **eə** / a diphthong in RP

Word	RP	Indian English
Walk	/ wɔ:k /	/ wɑ:k /
Talk	/ tɔ:k /	/ tɑ:k /
Form	/ fɔ:m /	/ fɑ:m /

- Indians use / ɑ ː / in the place of / ɔ ː / a diphthong in RP

The Consonant system of General Indian English:

As against the 24 consonantal phonemes of RP, GIE has a consonantal system consisting of 23 consonants. Some of the important variations are discussed below.

- Many Indians use the voiced labio-dental frictionless continuant / ʋ / in place of / **v** / and / **w** / which occurs in RP

Word	RP	Indian English
Arrive	/ ə'raiv /	/ ə'raiʋ /
Very	/ veri /	/ ʋeri /
Even	/ i:vn /	/ i:ʋn /

- Final / **v** / is omitted in Indian English

Word	RP	Indian English
Improve	/ im'pru:v/	/ im'pru: /
Twelve	/ twelv /	/ twel /

- Omission of / **j** / in Indian English

Word	RP	Indian English
Students	/ stju:dnts /	/ stu:dents /
Duty	/ dju:ti /	/ du:ti /

- General Indian English has dental plosives / **t̪** / and / **d̪** / instead of the RP dental fricatives / **θ** / and / **ð** /
- Indians tend to use / **t̪** / in the place of RP / **θ** /

Word	RP	Indian English
Thanks	/ θæŋks/	/ t̪æŋks /
Teeth	/ ti: θ /	/ t̪i: t̪ʰ /

Indians tend to use / **d̪** / in the place of RP / **ð**/

Word	RP	Indian English
That	/ ðæt /	/ d̪æt /
Brother	/ brʌðə /	/ brʌd̪ə/

- The intrusion of a vowel before a syllabic consonant

Word	RP	Indian English
Film	/ film /	/ filim /
Little	/ litl /	/ litil /

Indians use / **z** / in the place of RP / **s** /

Word	RP	Indian English
Purpose	/ pɜ:pəs /	/ pɜ:pəz /
House	/ həʊs /	/ həʊz /

RP has three pairs of plosive Phonemes

/p,b/ bilabial

/t,d/ alveolar RP is often retroflex in Indian English [t, ɖ]

/k,g/ velar

/p,t,k/ are voiceless and relatively strong called fortis; /b,d, g/ are voiced and relatively weak- lenis

In British R.P. /p,t,k/ at the start of accented syllables are aspirated, that's a powerful puff of breath after the discharge of the plosive before the subsequent vowel begins, e.g.,

Pack [phæk], table ['ʈheɪb], cage [kheɪ dʒ]

This aspiration does not occur in Indian English; due to lack of aspiration could be a frequent reason behind Indian English being unintelligible to native speakers. It's desirable to possess some aspiration in /p,t,k/ once they occur initially in accented syllables.

It's desirable to possess some aspiration in /p,t,k/ once they occur initially in accented syllables.

In Indian English /k/ is un-aspirated altogether positions. It's necessary to aspirate it at the start of accented syllables when reproving native English speakers; otherwise, there's an opening of confusion between pairs like cold and gold, cot and got.

Conclusion

Indian English spoken throughout the Subcontinent is vibrant, varies from region to region, and follows its own rules of development. The various dialects of English spoken even within the country underscore the unique languages and cultures of the people who speak them. Thus, I think that we want not to worry about imitating the British accent completely for we are Indians and our dialect will predominate. Also, it's not awkward for that's our identity but should make sure to pronounce the word correctly to the extent that it doesn't create confusion within the mind of the listener and different letters within the word will be distinguished.

It's concluded that there are some distinctive varieties of pronunciation between Indian English and British English.

Works Cited

Bansal, R. K.,(1976). *The Intelligibility of Indian English*, Monograph No. 4, Second (abridged) edition, CIEFL, Hyderabad

Bansal, R.K. (1969). *The Intelligibility of Indian English*, Monograph No.4 Orient Longman Ltd: Madras.

Brutt. Griffler. Janina. (2002). *World English: A Study of its Development*. Multilingual Matter

Ltd, Australia.

Caford, J.C. (1977) *Fundamental problems in Phinetics*, Edinburgh University Press

Catford, J.C. (1950). *Intelligibility. English Language Teaching*, Vol. 5. British Council: London.

Collins and Mees, (2002) *Practical Phonetics and Phonology*; a resource book for students. London and New York: Rutledge.

Crystal, David. (1988). the *English Language.* Penguin Books. Ltd. London.

Das, K. (1973). Cited in Kachru,B.B. (ed.) (1986). *The Alchemy of English -The Spread Functions and Models of Non- native Englishes.* Pergamon Press Ltd:

Oxford.

Dhamjia, P.V. and J. Seth. (1979). A *Course in Phonetics and Spoken English,* Prentice Hall of India Private Ltd.

Gimson, A.C. (1980). *An Introduction to the Pronunciation of English,* Edward Arnold: London.

Hooke, R. and Trudgill, P. (1987) *A Handbook of English Pronunciation,* London: Edward Arnold

Kreidler, C . W. (1989) *The Pronunciation of English,* Oxford: Blackwell

Ladeoged Peter, (1975) *A course in Phonetics, United State of America*: Harcourt Brace Jovanovich, Inc.

O'Connor, J. D. (1980) *Better English Pronunciation,* 2nd edition, Cambridge University Press

Works Cited

- **Mr. Bhaskara Rao Chintha** has been working as an Assistant Professor of English for 2 years in the Department of Humanities & Sciences, at St. Martin's Engineering College (Autonomous), Dhulapally, Secunderabad, Telangana, India. He has been teaching English for more than 12 years in various engineering colleges in Hyderabad. He cleared AP-SET (2013) in English. He obtained M.A. in English from Acharya Nagarjuna University, Guntur & he earned Post Graduation Diploma in Teaching of English (PGDTE) from EFLU, Hyderabad. He has published 4 research papers in UGC Care & reputed International journals. He presented 3 research papers at International Virtual Conferences. During Covid-19, he has participated in several Conferences, FDPs, Webinars & Workshops. His research interests are ESP, ESL teaching and Phonetics.

CHAPTER IX

HOW ELT MECHANISM WORKS ON DIFFERENTLY ABLED?

Shincy C. Joy
Ph. D. Research Scholar
SRM University, Andra Pradesh

ABSTRACT

For intermediate and advanced level students with learning disabilities, there is no one-size-fits-all method for teaching English as a foreign language. Despite this, research suggests these learners do well at decoding but lack the cognitive and metacognitive skills necessary for language comprehension and production. In order to help students with learning disabilities take advantage of experimental, reflective learning processes, effectively modelled cognitive processes must be incorporated into learning strategies instruction. In addition, the innovation and inclusion of technology and the learning experience have indeed contributed positively to this aspect. By carrying out this study, the researcher aims to shine a light on the importance of developing an effective learning methodology that is time-efficient and can help create a sense of understanding between the speaker and the listener, especially the ELT language learning in better patient understanding by nurses in health centres.

Keywords: ELT, Differently Abled People, Language Learning,

Introduction

Language is the primary means of communication, where words and sentences make for the key elements.

Any student learning a new language is introduced to the grammatical structure of the sentences, especially when training through worksheets and exercises. The learning experience is guided by a tutor, where the teacher's guidance and instructions regarding the exercises help the students learn better, where they reproduce and repeat the teaching patterns (Canon 437). According to records, there are fifty to three hundred typical sentence patterns that can be used for a training process, and essentially, this system of a large number of training processes is inefficient for a learner of a new language. It takes a long time to be proficient over a particular language learning system to be established. As specialists point out, it is vital to have a fundamental language structure within a limited duration or short-term constraint for feasible language maintenance in their respective fields.

Moreover, it is imperative to be understood that learning a foreign language should be effortless and should not exceed a time of more than one or two years. Learning a language should not be a hindrance but something that can aid the individual in acquiring skills without spending long hours and even years on the same. Above all, speech in any language is made up of a set of Elementary phrases. It remains an unconscious mystery to the speaker when it is connected with sentence structures. Nevertheless, for most cases, it is the structure that is being the hurdle for a foreign learner in a new language situation; because while building a sentence in a foreign language, students make analogies with their mother tongue. It causes or abounds boundless mistakes when dealing with complex utterances.

It sounds unproductive and feels withdrawal from new language learning. A scientific study of language learning has been introduced and proposed a proper and viable solution for these phenomena. The idea was first introduced by the language teachers at a Russian teachers' training college viz. Riga (Freeman & Freeman 14-20). However, it remained obscure to the public. They are learning the elementary structure of several foreign languages made possible by a newly developed learning method in mere twelve hours. As aforementioned, all the languages are means of communication, and their key elements are simple sentences that contain hidden components commonly applicable to all languages. Ultimately, in any language people talk about -somebody a specific action or particular object of an action.

For instance, the sentence " I am writing a letter ". Here one can observe the subject, or the action doer is "I ", and the object or the effect of the performer goes to the object "letter ", or as the object of action, and the linguistic action is "am writing ". Thus, there are three components in this sentence. It is what is called combinability that decides the appropriate type of simple sentence in different languages. Same as this, three components can be found in a sentence. In some cases, one or two of them may be missing. Specific sentences there may have only linguistic components in the absence of subject and object of the action. Hence, sentences can follow several patterns depending on the combinability of their components. For brevity, _" Sa"_ can be designated the *subject* of the action, _" Oa" the *object* of the action and "A"_ for the *action* itself. Thus, a sentence can have the following combinability. That is,

Sa + Oa.

Sa+ A+ Oa.

-A +Oa.

-A-

By circumstances, a learner or a student faces multiple tasks such as appreciating three components assimilating their combinability and deciding how this combinability is conveyed by studying the language. While the new learning process goes on, the native language comparison can have a positive role here. The learner can compare the combinability of the three components and their expression in his mother tongue and his currently studying language. Consequently, at the next level of language study, it can be applied with the newly developed habits in their "living" speech by the learned vocabulary or elementary materials, about certain specific topics such as "My Working Day " , "All About Me" etc.

Over time, the student or the learner gains the ability to construct oral sentences. Citing the example of classes based on this procedure have been conducted with beginners at Riga college of teachers' training in the University of Moscow. At a survey done in English, just over fifty per cent of all answers were correct, when one-third of students attempted in German, but the result was relatively low, and a pretty unfamiliar language for them, also had applied in French. At the end of the 12-hour course, the student-constructed sentences in all three languages almost without any mistakes. The primary aim of this teaching method is to gain the practical and immediate formation of speech habits in several languages. By applying this language learning methodology, the students will develop an interest in the subject (Rasna, Wayan & Tantra 1229). Moreover, when nurses deal with foreign language-speaking patients, a more efficient ETL can enable better conversation and understanding, thereby creating a better environment for the differently-abled individuals and the people working with them.

Literature Review

Language learning may be a constant method that begins at birth and continues. Language learning is a functioning cycle by which individuals foster their language abilities to utilize them successfully in their public activity, just as in their expert life. Through language learning, individuals can communicate their thoughts, opinions, information, experiences and feelings and learn to perceive themselves and understand others. They even establish their relationships with the members of their family, friends and others. Young learners enhance their language learning skills by utilizing what they grasp in additional advanced and novel contexts and with a more accelerated sophistication. To accumulate good communication in any language, one should get a decent command of the four language talents, i.e., listening, speaking, reading and writing.

Talking is viewed as the primary expertise among these four abilities, as correspondence is imperative in our day-to-day existence. In learning these four skills well, switching over to speaking skills is essential as they play a crucial role. In this regard, it is apt to mention that oral language carries a community's values, customs, traditions, stories and beliefs. As the interest for speaking skills expands step by step, the students attempt to focus on these abilities as communication is the principal part of the present worldwide market (Entwistle 1-9). There is a requirement to advance students' speaking abilities in this situation, and it needs to begin from the study hall itself. Once the students leave their instructive organizations after they complete their investigations, they cannot gain proficiency with these talking abilities in a little while. Learning a language and getting dominance over speaking skills to require ordinary practice, and the classroom is the principal stage to gain all the abilities they need (Entwistle 8-20).

Henceforth the educators should show every one of the necessary abilities, mainly speaking abilities, to the students to foster their informative skills. Researchers point out that teachers should start simple and exciting activities that improve pupils' speaking skills at an early age, like, for example, transforming an affirmative sentence into a question, or an affirmative sentence into a negative sentence, for instance, to enhance the speaking skills of their students. If students are to learn how to speak a foreign language or a second language, they must master grammar and have a comprehensive vocabulary, which could enable better understanding between the speaker and the listener.

When speaking skills, both vocabulary and grammar proficiency play a crucial role in delivering the message appropriately for the context. Therefore, the biggest challenge for the learners is to combine keywords, phrases, sentences, etc., correctly to communicate (Chien 1-7) effectively. Researchers studying task-based pedagogy have found that the outcome of the learning process greatly depends on the interaction between a learner, a task, and a task situation. As part of the communicative language approach, which became popular in the early 1980s, English is being taught to emphasize communicative ability over the last two decades. Furthermore, within this communicative approach, Task-Based Language Teaching (TBLT) is widely used. TBLT combines several components: goals, procedures, and specific learning goals. Studies show that nursing students have found task-based language teaching, which uses simulations to train them in nursing English, a very engaging learning method (Kailani, Ahmad & Tenny 28-40).

Different countries define learning disabilities differently. In Australia, the term refers to a very narrow subgroup within the broader category of learning disabilities. According to the American lexicon, learning disabilities refer to various disorders characterized by considerable difficulty acquiring and applying to listen, speaking, reading, writing, reasoning, and math abilities. In Canada, learning disability refers to a range of disorders affecting acquiring, retaining, comprehending, organizing, or utilizing verbal and non-verbal information. Teaching English as a foreign language to students with learning disabilities at the intermediate and advanced levels does not follow a specific formula. However, research shows that these students are proficient in decoding, but they have difficulty comprehending and producing language because they lack effective cognitive and metacognitive strategies.

Research shows that is critical that students with learning disabilities become strategic learners in order to utilize the learning strategies and techniques they have developed on their own effectively, instead of acting haphazardly and implementing whatever learning techniques they have designed for themselves, as their particular learning disabilities necessitate these tactics (Astuti 3021). Different teaching strategies are used for students with and without disabilities. Special teaching strategies are required for disabled students. Many strategies do not suit disabled students. After teachers understand their students' abilities and needs, they can select appropriate teaching strategies. A learning disability is defined as a problem with how the brain processes information. To assist students with learning disabilities to form effective, reflective learning processes, effective cognitive processes must, of course, be modelled through learning strategies instruction. It was evident that successful interventions for students with learning disabilities focus on helping students learn at intermediate and advanced levels.

Additionally, how to change ineffective and inefficient learning processes and enable them to become independent learners. Technology also plays a significant role in the process of learning a language. As we advance into the 21st century, technology is becoming increasingly available for language learning and teaching, and its use in classrooms worldwide is becoming just as important as the language itself (Motteram). As language skills are rooted in complex processes, instruction should strive to improve the underlying processes and strategies these students rely on to learn language skills to help them overcome their learning challenges. In particular, strategies for learning a language are fundamental to the process.

By engaging in language learning, learners can develop linguistic comprehension and production skills. In addition to enhancing self-efficacy, motivation, and self-confidence, learning strategies help develop self-efficacy, motivation, and self-confidence. Also, learning strategies instruction aids learners in discovering what particular strategies work for them in various situations, which develops their ability to control their learning. Self-regulated learners also employ cognitive and metacognitive learning strategies. Studies have shown that students who use effective strategies can operate outside the classroom, where teacher guidance is not present, as lifelong learning is facilitated by effective learning strategies (El-Koumy 20). Nevertheless, this may not be valid for every differently-abled individual.

Need for the Study

While there are numerous ELT mechanisms and language learning methodologies, many methodologies pose a limitation. Although it sounds contradicting, the large number of methodologies can make it complex to choose an effective one that can be generally applied. Moreover, the plethora of teaching methods can be time-consuming, often causing the learners to lose interest, hindering effective learning. By carrying out this study, the researcher aims to shine a light on the importance of developing an effective learning methodology that is time-efficient and can help create a sense of understanding between the speaker and the listener. In a more profound sense, the study will look into the role of ELT language learning in better patient understanding by nurses in health centres.

Aim

To understand the ELT mechanism and its effectiveness on differently-abled people.

Objectives

The objectives of the study are as follows:

- To explore the ELT mechanism and its effectiveness
- To understand the formation of speech habits in different languages
- To analyze the practical application of language learning methodology in promoting better learning of a foreign language
- To understand the role of ELT language learning in better patient understanding by nurses in health centres

Methodology

According to Clifford Woody (2010), research is an academic activity that defines and redefines problems, formulating a hypothesis, collecting, organizing and evaluating data, deducing it, and reaching conclusions. The current study makes use of the qualitative research method. The idea of qualitative research deals with different knowledge claims, research methods, and the various data collection methods and analysis tools employed for the investigation. Qualitative data can be derived and accumulated from observations, interviews, surveys and questionnaires, documented texts, and the researcher's thoughts and feedback. For the current study, the researcher can apply the survey research method to understand the ELT mechanism and its effectiveness on differently-abled people. The study respondents for the research can be nurses or doctors who work with differently-abled people.

Contribution of the Study

By carrying out this study, the researcher aims to understand the complexities involved in ETL language learning methodologies. Exploring understanding the same would aid learners and tutors in the ETL setting. Moreover, the study also holds the potential of creating a practical framework that could help ETL learners better acquire the language and facilitate better communication and understanding.

Works Cited

1. Caon, F. (2020). Motivation, Pleasure and a Playful Methodology in Language Learning. Educazione Linguistica. Language Education.
2. El-Koumy, Abdel Salam. "Teaching English as a foreign language to students with learning disabilities at the

intermediate and advanced levels: a multiple-strategies approach." *Revised Edition (February 20, 2020). Published by Dar An-Nashr for Universities, Cairo, Egypt, Revised Edition* (2020).

3. Entwistle, Noel. "University teaching-learning environments and their influences on student learning: An introduction to the ETL Project." *EARLI conference, Padova*. 2003.
4. Entwistle, N. J., et al. "Teaching and learning analogue electronics in undergraduate courses: preliminary findings from the ETL project." *International Journal of Electrical Engineering Education* 42.1 (2005): 8-20.
5. Larsen-Freeman, Diane, and Donald Freeman. "Language moves: The place of "foreign" languages in classroom teaching and learning." Review of Research in Education 32.1 (2008): 147-186.
6. Larsen-Freeman, Diane, and Donald Freeman. "Language moves: The place of "foreign" languages in classroom teaching and learning." *Review of Research in Education* 32.1 (2008): 147-186.
7. Kailani, Ahmad, and Tenny Murtiningsih. "Teaching English for nursing by using task-based language teaching." International Journal of Educational Best Practices 3.2 (2019): 28-40.
8. Motteram, Gary. *Innovations in learning technologies for English language teaching*. British Council, 2013.
9. Rasna, I. Wayan, and Dewa Komang Tantra. "Reconstruction of local wisdom for character education through the Indonesia language learning: An Ethno-pedagogical methodology." Theory and Practice in Language Studies 7.12 (2017): 1229-1235.

CHAPTER X

NEW LAND TENURE POLICY OF TRAVANCORE AND THE BEGINNING OF RECLAMATIONS IN KUTTANADU

Nandu.P. Kumar
Ph. D. Research Schoar
PG and Research Department of History
N.S.S. Hindu College, Perunna, Changanassery, Kerala.

Introduction

The 19th century was a turning point in the history of Kuttanadu like other parts of Travancore because this period marks the beginning of reclamations in the entire part of Travancore. There are a lot of changes that took place in Kuttanadu during this period but this paper focuses on major changes in the land tenure system of 19th-century Kuttanadu, how it paved the way for reclamations and also examines how these policies affected the socio-economic life of Kuttanadu. Agriculture was the major occupation of Kuttanadu, the *pattam* declaration in 1818 by the Travancore state government not only changed the economic pattern of the society but also had a deep influence on the social-cultural aspect society. The immediate economic change in Kuttanadu after the declaration of *pattam* proclamation is the land reclamations. Land reclamation is a process by which the marshy areas of backwaters were converted for farming, especially for rice cultivation. As a result of this, the low water level regions of Vembanad Lake were reclaimed and made for rice cultivation.

According to the government, it was policy to increase agrarian lands and productivity. In 1818, the government issued a royal proclamation with the view to encourage the cultivation of wastelands and making permanent improvements inland by guaranteeing the enjoyment of land tax-free for the first ten years and imposing only a light tax thereafter and recognizing for post improvements on newly reclaimed land.[i] As the result of this a group of landholding communities were emerged and later they became the strong supporters of the then Travancore Government. Like other parts of Travancore, there is also a group of landholding communities that emerged as the result of land reclamations in Kuttanadu too, these groups mainly constituted *Syrian Christians*, *Nairs* and *Namboothiri Brahmanas*. So these groups were commonly considered as an upper or middle class during that period. Even though these communities constituted the majority of farming lands but the law of inheritance and other factors changed according to caste and religious norms.

THE NEWLY EMERGING LANDHOLDERS OF 19TH CENTURY KUTTANADU

The landholding communities of 19th century Kuttanadu are commonly categorized under the category of the upper and middle-class sections in that period. In Kuttanadu majority were poor agricultural labourers and who lead a very miserable life, here actual workers were not the owners of the land. The land-owning minority convert the majority of the working class into a cheap labour force and use them for their agrarian activities and also gains maximum profit. Early landowners of the land particularly were *Bhramins* who holds land under *Janmam rights*. The higher sections of the society especially *Syrian Christians, Nairs, Brahmins* belonged to the minority in numbers but hold ownership of the majority of the land. Working sections of the society mainly belong to the backward communities particularly from *Ezhavas*, *Parayas* and *Pulayas*. The *pattam proclamation* leads to the increase of the land reclamation process as a result of this the low tide regions of upper and lower Kuttanadu came under paddy cultivation. The *Syrian Christians* and *Nairs* were considered as the major land reclaimers in that period and the lower sections became the working sections for this process. As the result of land reclamation, agricultural production was increased and the surplus was sent to market. This was considered as a typical example for the commercialisation of agriculture as the life of landholders became prosperous at the same time majority of workers became marginalized and live under miserable conditions. This economic prosperity leads to changes in cultural aspects of these sections in the society.

The rigidity of the caste system remained as one of the major obstacles to the social and economic changes in Travancore. So as the part of Travancore Kuttanadu did not differ from the existing nature of the hierarchical caste system which has a great influence on the land tenure pattern of Kuttanadu. By the middle of the 19th century out of the total population, *Nairs* and their subgroups accounted for 30%, Syrian Christians 12%, *Muslims* 5%, *Ezhavas* 15%, *Shannars* 6% and the slave castes 30%.[ii] The *Bhramins* considered themselves as the custodian of temples and viewed agricultural work as a disgraceful profession. *Nairs* commonly belongs to the warrior community and are also engaged in administration activities. They also viewed the agrarian sector as a profession for low-class people. *Nairs* and *Brahmins*, who owned a sizeable portion of cultivatable land leased out the land to the tenants belonging to the other castes. Thus landownership was vested in a minority of landholders who had no interest in agriculture. But this system got certain structural changes after the adaptation of new economic policy and Reclamations.

The next important obstacle for the agrarian sector was the practice of the Matrilineal system of inheritance (*Marumakathayam*) followed by *Nairs*. This is because Nairs were major landholders after Brahmanas in Kuttanadu and they follow the female inheritance of properties commonly known as *Marumakathayam*. A Matrilineal joint family is commonly called *Taravadu*. One of the main features of this type of inheritance is that the duty to manage the property right is vested with the elder male member of the family. Gross mismanagement of the *Taravadu* property was a common thing and there were constant feuds between members of *Taravadu* approaching civil courts. The younger and more enterprising were not given more opportunities for the management *Taravadu* landed property.

But later by the adaptation of the new economic policy in Travancore and starting of Reclamation, also paved the way for certain minute changes in the matrilineal system. But however, they were not at all competent with the Syrian Christians in the case of Reclamation especially because of practising the system of *Marumakathayam*. For certain families, this was different even though they followed the Matrilinieal system of inheritance but they were actively involved in the reclamation process. One of the important merits of *Marumakathayam* is that the Nair communities who actively engaged in the reclamation process compared to Syrian Christians were overpasses in the field of higher education. The increased paddy production which followed after reclamation increased the wealth of these families. Syrian Christians mainly follow a Patriarchal system of inheritance so they regularly invest their profit other business activities but in the case of Nair joint families the family business was mainly agriculture and which was controlled by the elder male member of the family and other male members were got much free time and the profit was used for their education. This resulted in the emergence of the newly educated class from these joint families, whose contributions were mainly concentrated in the social, cultural and religious reformations in the society.

THE CHANGING LAND TENURE SYSTEM OF 19TH CENTURY KUTTANADU

The land tenure system in Kuttanadu is very complex in nature. Land tenure policies adopted by the Travancore state government were favourable to the promotion and expansion of agriculture. By the end of the 18th century due to the annexation of territories belonging to conquered chieftains, about one half of the total cultivatable land came under state ownership and was known as *Pandaravaka* land. In 1812 with the acquisition of landed properties belonging to 378 wealthy temples, at the instance of Dewan Jhon Munro, resulted in the conversion of more than 1 lack acres of private lands into *sirkar* land, thereby bringing out a little less than a two-third of the cultivated area under the direct ownership of the state.[iii] The *Pandaravaka* lands were grouped as *Pattam, Otti, Inam* and *Viruthi*. The rest of the lands were under the categories of *Janmom* viz. freehold, tax-free lands and land paying *Rajyabhogam*. The freehold lands were held by members of the relatives of the royal families and Rajas, the second category belongs to temples (*Devasams*) and Bhramins (*Brahmasams*), and the third category belongs to various Christians and others.[iv]

During the early decades of the 19th century, Travancore took certain measures to increase agricultural productivity through the expansion of agrarian lands. As a result of this land, reclamations were held in several parts of Travancore especially in Kuttanadu. So after the *Pattam* proclamation and the land reclamations, several structural changes took place in the land tenure system of Kuttanadu. These measures had created opportunities for those who had sufficient capital for the conversion of wastelands into cultivatable lands without any restrictions of his caste or creed. The first beneficiaries of this measure in Kuttanadu were *Syrian Christians* and *Nairs*. *Syrian Christians* possessed a vast amount of liquid cash which they accumulated from the profit of the trade. In the case of *Nairs* it was different they were major administrative community in the government so they got the majority of the land as grants from the government for their valuable service to the throne so some of the

ambitious generations from this particular community also engaged in the reclamations became the masters of vast paddy fields in then Kuttanadu. At the latter, some *Ezhavas* also followed this same way. The next important measure which was taken by the government to increase agricultural production was the conferment of more rights to the tenants holding *Padaravaka* lands. Under *Pandaravaka system* there are two types of tenures are available one is *pattam* and the other is *Otti*. Tenure of *Otti* was considered as a privileged land tenure system as compared to *pattam* tenure, it is because it holds the right of transfer of occupancy. But the majority of tenure existed in the Travancore during that period mostly *pattam* tenure. This category of tenants increased gradually increased with the increasing no of the population but there is no improvement in the case of transfer rights etc. Except for the power to transfer the right of compensation for improvements, the tenants did not enjoy any other rights such as proprietary rights. This created a stagnant situation in which the land doesn't have value beyond the crops it produced. Travancore government also faced much difficulty in collecting land revenue dues since nobody is willing to purchase this land. In order to solve the stagnant situation, the government issued a *pattam* proclamation in 1865, which conferred full ownership rights on tenants subject to due payment of land revenue and removed all restrictions with respect to the transfer of ownership.

The measurement policies took over by the Travancore state government in the case of *pandaravaka* lands, the cash began to use widely for the transfer of land rights, thereby enhancing the circulation of cash in a hitherto stagnant non-monetised agricultural economy. This had created opportunities for certain communities especially *Syrian Christians* who had interests in trade and have capital with them to purchase land for cultivation. This changed economic situation created a peasant proprietary class who sell or purchase lands freely, this begins the emergence of the land market. This also marked the beginning stage of commercialisation of agriculture in the second half of the 19th century, of which *kayal krishi* in Kuttanadu and cash crops cultivation in high ranges were the best examples.

Encouragement from the side of the state government for the land reclamation in Kuttanadu was also a major concern for this study. As Kuttanadu both upper and lower regions is blessed with backwaters is given the scope for the reclamation of backwaters and which directly led to the expansion of paddy cultivation in Kuttanadu. The land reclamations were considered as an effort of full process which needs a lot of money and needs a large amount of working force for this process. Backwaters had to be reclaimed by constructing enclosing bund around the cultivation blocks, followed by draining of enclosed area, levelling the ground, constructing drainage of the irrigation channels and also from small bunds from inside the block. Reclamation had started as early as 1834.[v]

But the active encouragement from the side of the government begins only in the 1860s. There are certain measures taken over by the government to encourage the reclamation, first and the important one is the tax concession for the first five years. Loans were also given to the cultivators in view of the enormous capital expenditure required for the reclamation of the land. The government granted more concessions for reclamation of land by regulation in 1899. And the beginning of the 20th century about 5,500 acres of land had been reclaimed from the Vembanad Lake.[vi] During the 1880s 6 reclamation schemes were implemented by the state with the objective of changing the watercourses. These reclamation schemes are intended to bring more land under cultivation and also made actions to improve the yield of existing paddy fields. One of the major challenges faced by the farmers in the newly reclaimed land is constructing barriers to prevent the entry of brackish water from the lakes and seas. The government granted more concessions for the reclamation of the land by reclamation of 1899. And by the beginning of the 20th century, about 5,500 acres of land had been reclaimed from the Vembanad Lake.[vii]

Though the land tenure measure implemented by the Travancore were helpful for agricultural development especially in Kuttanadu it didn't result in an equitable distribution of the land. Even after the conferment of the ownership right to the tenants of *pandaravaka* land by *Pattam Proclamation* of 1865, about 25% of cultivatable remained as *Janmam lands* and actually cultivated by tenants at will. The *pandaravaka* lands were largely held by rich tenants who usually sublet them to the tenants-at-will for cultivation. By the beginning of the 20th century, it was estimated that about nine-tenths of the wetlands in Travancore was actually cultivated by tenants-at-will who take land on oral lease, *Pathivaram.*[viii] As the reclamation of the land was an expensive activity only rich people can enter in that activity, except this upper and a small no of middle-class people. So the remaining majority were either tenants-at-will, agricultural labourers or small farmers.

CONCLUSION

By the beginning of the 19th century the economy of Kuttanadu was backward in nature but later some years the agrarian economy of Kuttanadu began to change. This is because the adaptation of new economic policy and the beginning of land reclamations in Travancore directly influenced this region. The scarcity of rice forced the Travancore authority to adopt measures to increase rice production; the evolution of reclamations was one of the examples of these policies. As the result, the government give sanctions for wealthy people of Kuttanadu to conduct reclamation process in the low tide regions of Kuttanadu and brings these lands under paddy cultivation. So this process is commonly known as *Kayal Krishi* or wetland farming. Available evidence suggested that Travancore exported rice till about the 1840s. This is only because of the abundance of rice produced as the result of the new economic policy adopted by the Travancore. In this fortune, Kuttanadu has a key role to play because it became a rice bowl for Travancore as the result of reclamation and wetland farming. Major economic change in the case of Kuttanadu after the land reclamation was the change in the mode of production. In this particular case, the subsistent agrarian economy changed into a market-oriented economy. The history of commercialisation of agriculture of Kuttanadu begins from here. There were several obstacles against this transformation, the factors such as land-tenuership, the rigidity of the caste system and the practice of Matrilinity came under this category.

In the case of land ownership, the majority of the land was vested in the hands of Brahmins. According to the agricultural activities were considered as a bad profession so they were not interested in farming. So other castes mostly engaged in farming activities. Brahmins got *Janmam* right for the land they possessed. They give their land for cultivation under *Pattam* provision. During the early years of the 19th century, there were some measures taken by the state government to increase paddy cultivation in Travancore. But they already know that there were certain obstacles in their path. Among them the most important one was the Royal proclamation of 1818 in a view to bringing the majority of the wastelands under cultivation and giving fee concessions to those who act in this process. It directly leads to the beginning of land reclamations in Kuttanadu especially in the law tide regions of the Vembanad Lake.

Another important action from the side of the government was the *pattam* proclamation of 1865, which was a turning point in the economical history of Travancore. This act conferred full ownership rights on tenants subject to the due payment of land revenue and removed all restrictions with the transfer of ownership.

As per these new changes land tenure policy, there are some minute structural changes that happened in the entire land tenure system of Kuttanadu. One of the important changes was the emergence of new land- magnets, who are mainly constituted from *Syrian Christians*, *Nairs* and Some people from the *Ezhava* community. This means anyone who had cash in their hand can buy or exchange their land without any caste restriction, which marks the beginning of the land markets in Travancore. Newly emerged who were considered as major reclaimers of the 19th century Kuttanadu.

The new economic policy which was adopted by the Travancore state Government was mainly from the colonial influence and also from the internal need within the society, especially from political and economical needs. Mostly it was believed that it was from the pressure from British authority that Travancore started reclamation in high lands. In that period most of the forests were cleared for the farming of the cash crops such as rubber and other plantation crops. In the case of rice cultivation, it was different the scarcity of food grains lead the Travancore government to rethink the reclamation of marshy lands in Travancore, especially Kuttanadu. Anyhow the real agenda of the Government is to nature an elite group of landholders to support the political authority of Travancore. But the changes were only in the top layer of the society and the majority of the marginalized section also became more oppressed. At the beginning of the 19th century, Kuttanadu witnessed certain changes mostly in the land tenure system mostly in favour of reclamations and finally leads to the emergence of a market-based economy.

END-NOTES

[1] Royal Proclamation Of 993 ME (AD 1818) Cited in Travancore Land Revenue Manual, 1915, Vol-IV, P.229.

ii Prakash, B.A, Economic History of Kerala From 1800 to 1947 AD Part ii Travancore, Trivandrum Economic Studies Society.

iii Vargheese T.C, 1970, Agrarian Change and Economic Consequences: Land Tenures in Kerala 1850-1960, Allied Publishers, Bombay, P.30.

Iv Ibid, P.31.

V Velupillai T.K, Travancore State Manual Vol.iii, P.12.

Vi Pillai V.R and Panickar P.G.K, Land Reclamation in Kerala, Asia Publishing House, Bombay.

vii Pillai V.R and Panickar P.G.K Land Reclamation in Kerala, Asia Publishing House, Bombay.

Viii Nagam Aiya V, 1906, The Travancore State Manual, Vol. iii, P. 150.

Works Cited

1. Agur, C.M, *Church History of Travancore*, Asian Educational Service, Madras, 1990.
2. Aiya, V, Naga, *Travancore State Manual*, Travancore Government Press, Trivandrum, 1906.
3. Balakrishnan, E, *History of communist movements in Kerala*, KurushetraPrakasan, Eranakulam, 1988.
4. Beiteille, Andre, *Studies in Agrarian Social Structure*, New Delhi, OUP, 1983.
5. Bose, Chandra, Satheesh and Varghese, ShyamShiju(Ed), *Kerala Modernity: Ideas, Spaces, and practises in Transition,* Orient Black Swan, New Delhi, 2015.
6. Cherian, P.J(Ed), *Essays on the Cultural Formation of Kerala,* Kerala Gazetteers Department, Trivandrum, 1999.

7. Cherian, P.J(Ed), *Perspectives on Kerala History*, Kerala State Gazetteer, Vol – 2, Trivandrum, 1999.
8. Guha Ranajith, *A subaltern Studies Reader,1986-1995*, University of Minnesota Press,1997.
9. Gurukal, Rajan and Variyer, Raghava (Ed), *Cultural History of Kerala*, Department of Cultural Publications, Trivandrum, 1999.
10. Jeffrey, Robin, *Decline of Nair Dominance: Society and Politics in Travancore: 1847-1908*, Sussex University Press, New Delhi, 1979.
11. Kamalasanan, N, K, *Kuttanadum Keralathile KarshakathozhilaliPrasthanavum*, D.C Books, Kottayam, 1993.
12. Menon, Sreedhara A, *A Survey of Kerala History*, DC Books,2007.
13. Mateer Samuel, *Native Life in Travancore*, Victoria Institutions, 1883.
14. Namboodiripad, EMS, *Reminiscences of an Indian Communist*, National Book Centre, New Delhi, 1989.
15. Pillai, V.R, and P.G.K, Panickar, *Land Reclamation in Kerala*, Asia Publishing House, 1965.
16. Pradhan, Sudhi(Ed), *Marxist Cultural Movement in India*, Vol-2, Nava, Calcutta, 1982.
17. Prakash, B.A, *Economic History of Kerala From 1800 to 1947 AD*, Part ii Travancore, Trivandrum Economic Studies Society.
18. *Royal Proclamation of 993 ME(AD 1818) Stated in Travancore State Manual*,1915, Vol-iv,P.229.
19. Sanal Mohan.P, *Modernity of Slavery: Struggles Against Caste Inequality in Colonial Kerala*, Oxford University Press,2015.
20. Taylor Charles, *Modern Social Imaginaries*, Critical Quest, New Delhi, 2009.

21. Varghese, TC, *Agrarian Changes and Economic Consequences*, Allied Publishers, Bombay, 1970.
22. Velupillai, T.K, *Travancore State Manual*, Trivandrum,
23. Williams, Raymond, *Materialism and Culture*, Vergo, London, 1980.

CHAPTER XI

WHEN THE PEOPLE CHANGE THE PALACE CANNOT HOLD: A CRITICAL ANALYSIS OF THE POWER BY NAOMI ALDERMAN

Aamina Akhtar

Research Scholar, Department of English, School of Languages,

Linguistics and Indology, Maulana Azad National Urdu University, Hyderabad.

***When the people change, the palace cannot hold*: A Critical Analysis of The Power by Naomi Alderman**

Abstract

Since time immemorial gender issues have always been an apple of discord between different critics. Some have even come up with the idea that a lot of differences could end if women become the leaders of the world. Naomi Alderman's novel, *The Power* makes women the dominant gender, as such the binary opposition of gender roles: dominant-submissive; are being deconstructed. The novel, science fiction, is about a future where women are empowered with the ability to release electrical jolts from their fingers, torture and kill men with a touch. Naomi Alderman has depicted an image of the world where women get violent towards men. The author has beautifully presented how the behaviour of women around the world gets increasingly sadistic. The paper analyzes Naomi Alderman's *The Power* in the light of Butler's 'Gender Performativity' concept; in which she has collapsed the distinction of sex and gender and concludes that 'gender is not something one is, it is something one does, an act, or rather more precisely, a sequence of acts, a verb rather than a noun, a doing rather than a being.' The study also aims at exploring the role of power in turning the world upside down.

Keywords: Science Fiction, Gender, Power, Violence, Naomi Alderman

Introduction

"*Gender is a shell game. What is a man? Whatever a woman isn't. What is a woman? Whatever a man isn't. Tap on it and it's hollow. Look under the shells: it's not there*" (325).

The novel is about a future where women are empowered with the ability to release electric jolts from their fingers to torture and kill men with a touch. Some theorists believe if women are given power, society would become egalitarian in all respects. But the novelist counters this view in the novel by presenting a world where women could go to any extent to insult men. In the novel, there is a world where women start to develop a muscle called 'skein', which provides them with a huge amount of power to hurt others by sending them severe electric shocks. The author also portrays 'how the ability to inflict violence on others imbues individuals with power, which can then expand into politics, religion, and economic influence.

The Article, A Feminist Analysis of the Fictional Novel *The Power*, in which a feministic analysis has been conducted on this book by Akhtar Ali, Rafique Ahmed et al in 2021. This research; identifies that women also have the potentials and capabilities to compete with men in every sphere of life and justifies it with reference to Selma James feminist theory. This research focuses only on the positive side of women.

The paper, ' *Feminism in the Power*', by Syed Fizza Anwar Shah, Dr Mirza Naveed et. published in the European Journal of Gender Studies in 2021, focused on women's desires for complete freedom from their patriarchy and equality with men on every ground in real life. They have analyzed this novel from a feminist perspective only.

Sally Christina Slette in '*The war of the Sexes: Power Hierarchy and Gendered oppression in Atwood's The Handmaids Tale and Alderman's The Power'*, shows that both novels call attention to the way Christian Ideology advocates and upholds patriarchal gender norms and power hierarchies. She has also discussed how rape and the threat of rape serve to uphold the power dynamic between the sexes. Furthermore, she has also paid attention to the way power is ascribed to the construction of our social structures.

Constance Grady says in the Vox Book Club Newsletter about this novel that Alderman's narrative shows us what power looks like in action in different corners of the world. 'With the reversal of power, there comes intense and visceral defamiliarization of all the ways we unthinkingly gender power. All of the creepy old tropes that we are so used to get flipped on their heads.

Sophie Gilbert has said about Alderman's novel that the world of this book is 'richly imagined, ambitious, and propulsively written' where people jostle hustle and scrap and sell out each other to get ahead, no matter their gender. Mary Beard writes in her manifesto Women and Power from 2017 that if our understanding of power results in cruelty and sadism towards the less powerful gender, surely the solution is not merely that the victimized gender becomes the more powerful and vice versa. A change in the discourse of power is required, including a change in how we allow the powerful to feel entitled to act towards their subjects. It requires a more level playing field, where one is not more inherently powerful because of arbitrary categorization such as gender and gender expressions. Naomi Alderman discusses this conceptual issue with our discourse of power in The Power.

Pigmans writes that " Alderman has written our era's Handmaids Tale, and like Margaret Atwood's classic, The Power is one of those essential works that terrifies and illuminates, engages and encourages".

Research Objectives

The research or this paper aims to point out that:

Power can corrupt human beings equally.

Gender is just a label that is to be reduced into nothingness.

To what extent women can go once they become powerful

Research Questions

The paper is going to answer the following questions:

Is gender imbalance or power dynamics the cause of suffering?

What would happen to the world if women become its leaders?

How violent women could get to remain in the power?

Significance of the study:

The study is significant because it provides readers with an insight into what could or might happen when the patriarchal world is reversed and the gender binary concept is being deconstructed.

Research Method

The methodology is to be qualitative in nature. Textual analysis and Discourse analysis are the major components that are to be taken into consideration for character analysis and plot discussion.

Theoretical Perspective

According to Butler's, Gender Performativity concept – Gender is not what one is but it is what we do so it questions all the preconceived notions about gender. Butler says that our society labels ' an infant' at the very time of its existence which restricts a person to the role already set in the existing society which later on creates a lot of conflicts and differences between men and women and the society starts to look upon women as weaker than men which is not the case in reality. It's all about who would hold the power because both men and women could become violent once they become powerful. The same thing is being depicted in the novel and the paper analyses the novel from this very perspective. It will be analyzing the novel from the character-wise to reach the conclusion.

Textual Analysis

A patriarchal society is characterized by a difference in attitude towards men and women, often it's women who have been oppressed and suppressed by the dominant men population. It also evokes a belief that if women become equal to men physically then this gender imbalance would be reduced to a large extent. In this novel, where a world is presented in which men can't walk down the street at night without the company of women, as such women are given physical dominance, the author flips the concept of dominance and submission and the current power dynamics.

Just like a man, she says, does not know how to be silent, thinks we always want to hear what he has to say, always talking talking talking...(223)

She also says to him, this bottle is worth more than you. (223)

The following extract from the novel shows the dominating nature of a woman and how submissive and frightened men have become under their leadership. The lines talk about the corruption and viciousness of Tatiana Maskalov who has killed her husband with her power to become the president herself. When a man namely Peter interrupted her at a reception she becomes cruel and mistreats him bitterly. She drops the wine bottle on the floor and asks him to 'lick it up' and humiliate's him in front of everyone. The sharp pieces of glass hurt his throat and blood starts to flow out of the wound. Although his friends help him to extract those splinters out of his throat as he is in complete shock and starts crying 'from the shock and the shame and fear and the humiliation and the pain and what he has been subjected to'. Furthermore, she imposes such autocratic and unjust rules which curtail men's freedom to drive, travel, and work without the consent of a female guardian.

Enforcing rules like these procure more opportunities for women who then begin begun to rape, murder, and electrify men at will. Through Tatiana's character, Alderman conveys that female rulers can be just as corrupted as men, her way of enacting unjust laws mirrors those of the old patriarchal regime. Moreover, the novelist in the depiction of Tatiana's character counters the belief that it's not a question of opportunities where women could rule better than men but on the contrary, they would just behave the same way as men do in a patriarchal society. All this shows that the world's system can only change if the word 'gender' is crumbled or considered just a "performance" (Butler). *Power doesn't care who uses it*. (287)

Roxy, the daughter of don, becomes a symbol of the absolute power that everyone is afraid of in the novel. Although she doesn't seem as much corrupted as other characters in the novel, the novelist depicts her in a way that shows how powerful people can manipulate even religious people with their diplomacy. She manufactures the drug called ‘ Glitter' that enhances the power of women in the novel but later on this drug transmits into politics and religion as well. Through an incident that happened with his brother where he was raped and abused by two girls, the novelist tries to imply how even in the matriarchal society the victim is being held responsible for their actions. When being questioned why they do it to him, they responded, “he was asking for it. He begged us for it, wanted us to hurt him...and he is a little dirty boy” (190) So here Alderman emphasizes that blame game-narratives like these are never going to change even in the women-controlled world unless and until the gender concept won't end. *Young men tended to be too frightened. There was no point talking to women at all; even meeting their eyes felt too dangerous.* (255)

Tunde, a Nigerian Journalist, is one of the young and main male characters in the novel who suffers terribly under the atrocious rulership of women/ or a women-centred world. Although he is the first one who recognizes and documents the actions of women gaining power and puts it online nevertheless, he has been subjected to various horrors. Frequently it has been observed in our society that women live in constant fear because they are being considered weaker than men and have to endure various abuses at the hands of men based on a misinterpreted concept that men are their masters. But in the novel, a different scenario has been demonstrated in which men are seen becoming vulnerable and they are abused, raped, sacrificed in cultish ceremonies, and even murdered for no reason.

Alderman also showed how Tunde lives in constant trauma of ever getting close to any woman after being almost raped by a woman. As feminists claim that several great works of women have been stolen by men for which they received credit from people while their original authors(women) have been ignored but here in the novel Alderman showed how the same thing happened with Tunde. He got shocked after seeing his obituary in the newspaper. It is Nina, his friend whom he trusted blindly by sending all his materials such as photographs and interviews to keep them safe but she cheated him by stealing everything from him and publishing it under her name. After seeing all this Tunde let out a noise he had not known was in him. A bellow from the back of the throat. The sound of grieving. Deeper than sobs. Again Alderman implies that this could happen to the menfolk as well if the world would become matriarchal. And consequently, the world would become as difficult for men as it is currently for women. Alderman also points out that even reversing the roles won't be a solution for reducing the gender differences but we need to stop labelling the people. In reality, both men and women hold the same power so they can't be gendered by just their actions. *For the earth is filled with violence, and every living thing has lost its way.* (1)

Allie, a girl who kills her father because he uses to abuse and rape her continuously. Later on in the novel, she starts to teach her religion and calls herself Eve after becoming powerful. She even proceeds to rewrite the scripture and wants to keep only those parts that suit her narrative. Through her character Alderman indicated that faith and religion can be manipulated by powerful figures. Although she calls herself a very pious figure she becomes evil the moment someone starts to question her religion. She even kills some girls who tried to oppose her belief system. Women undergo a lot of crises and troubles on the religious ground in a patriarchal society only because men are the owners of some scriptures which also sometimes become the reason for gender differences. So Alderman denoted how they can be easily manipulated. So all these beliefs are socially constructed which can be eliminated if we take this issue seriously.

The shape of the power is always the same: It is infinite, it is complex, it is forever branching. While it is alive like a tree, it is growing; while it contains itself, it is a multitude. Its directions are unpredictable; it obeys its own laws (2). There's never been a right choice, honeybun. The whole idea that there are two things and you have to choose from is the problem. (309)

Your whole question is a mistake. Who's is the serpent and who's is the Holy Mother? Who's bad and who's good? Who persuaded the other one to eat the apple? Who has the power and who's powerless? All of these questions are the wrong question.

These lines from the novel exceptionally try to point out that once a person comes into power they never realize what it would compel them to do. They become violent, oppressive, unjust, and whatnot in their actions so power doesn't care who uses it whether a female or male it would spontaneously make them atrocious. Alderman wants to convey a message that perhaps the very question about the binary concept of weak and strong, superior and inferior are wrong because, in the end, we all are human beings so we should stop making differences between the genders.

Conclusion

In a patriarchal society, it has frequently been observed that because of the gender imbalance women have to suffer a lot at the hands of men which has implied that once the power dynamics are flipped it would end the sufferings of women. But what was found out after analyzing the novel is the other way round. This study ascertains that in the matriarchal system, it's men who have to suffer the same way as women do in patriarchy. This study has achieved the research objectives and has answered the questions by providing textual evidence from the novel. It has justified Butler's concept's relevance to the novel by showing that gender difference won't end whether it is patriarchy or matriarchy unless and until we take the word gender just as a performance and action. Through the characters of Tatiana, Roxy, Allie, it confirms that women can get violent to the extreme level once they become powerful. Eventually, the study establishes that nothing is going to change even after reversing the roles lest the gender itself gets dissolved into nothingness.

Works Cited

Alderman, N. (2017). *The Power.* Hachette UK

Jordan, Justine (2 November 2016). "The Power by Naomi Alderman review – if girls ruled the world". The Guardian. Retrieved 16 April 2018.

"The 10 Best Books of 2017". The New York Times. 30 November 2017. Retrieved 16 April 2018.

https://en.m.wikipedia.org/wiki/
The_Power_(Alderman_novel)

Grady, C. (2021). How Naomi Alderman's novel *The Power* deconstructs the patriarchy. *Vox Book Club newsletter.*

Gilbert, S (2017). What If Women Had *The Power.* The Atlantic

Dolmer, I A (2017). Would the world be a better place with women in charge? A literary analysis of Naomi Alderman's The Power.

Beard, M (2017). *Women and Power: A Manifesto.*

Salih, S. (2002). On Judith Butler and Performativity

Butler, J.(2002). Gender Trouble: *Feminism and the Subversion of Identity.* Routledge New York

https://criticallegalthinking.com/2016/11/14/judith-butlers-performativity/

https://cla.purdue.edu/academic/english/theory/genderandsex/modules/butlergendersex.html

https://www.waterstones.com/book/the-power/naomi-alderman/9780670919963

https://www.litcharts.com/lit/the-power

https://www.goodreads.com/book/show/29751398-the-power

https://www.coursehero.com/file/41665133/The-power-by-naomi-alderman/

CHAPTER XII

THE SURVIVING TALE OF DALITS IN BENGAL: THROUGH THE LENS OF SURVIVAL IN MY WORLD: GROWING UP DALIT IN BENGAL.

Sutadripa Dutta Choudhury
Ph. D. Research Scholar, Department of English,
St. Xavier's University, Kolkata, India.

ABSTRACT

The paper strives to analyse Surviving in My World: Growing Up Dalit in Bengal by Manohar Mouli Biswas as a Dalit autobiography and how it depicts the writer's life in a contentious community where he has been prone to inhumane suffering and intimidation imposed by the upper castes only for appearing from a Dalit background. Biswas's autobiographical novel lends readers a vent into the inhumane nature of suffering, both corporal and societal, inflicted upon the Dalits in Bengal. It is largely claimed by Dalit writers that non-Dalit writers can never communicate the suffering experienced by the Dalits through their writings as their writings come from a certain sense of sympathy but Dalit writers largely empathize with their experienced pain and can delineate it through their writings quite distinctly. This disparity formulates a huge rift between the perceptions of the Dalit writers and that of the non-Dalit writers. This is perhaps why the Dalit writers prefer to communicate their arguments through their autobiographies without any influence of any writer outside the Dalit community. My paper will thus serve as a mirror within our society where caste plays a pivotal evil role, formulating a rift. The experiences of Manohar Mouli Biswas not only make us reckon his hardships but also make us amazed at our society where people are treated as animals even though they are constantly trying to sustain their livelihood through adequate means. The paper will thereby exhibit how Dalit trajectories trundle to form a new world of literature in Bengal through the autobiography of Manohar Mouli Biswas.

• • •

The Surviving Tale Of Dalits In Bengal: Through The Lens Of Survival In My World:Growing Up Dalit In Bengal.

Introduction

According to scholars, the term "Dalit Literature" emanated in the year 1958, from the first meeting of the Maharashtra Dalit Sahitya Sangh. People often view the 1960s, and 1970s as the period of Dalit Literature emergence. However, the 1920s glowed the arrival of Dalit pamphlet literature which ensued at roughly the same time when B.R. Ambedkar had initiated his revolution of Dalit people being allowed inside Hindu temples.

A Dalit representation emerged for the first time in Marathi literature when the iconic work 'Jevha Mi JaatChorli' (When I had concealed my caste), was written by BaburaoBagul in the year 1963. Namdeo Laxman Dhasal, another Marathi Dalit activist, was inspired greatly by Bagul's works. He steered the Dalit literary world numerous gems from the 1970s. Dhasal, alongside J.V. Pawar, and Arun Kamble, founded the Dalit Panthers in

1972. The organisation is taken to be one of the major path-breakers in the Dalit revolution. It has endorsed by the ideologies of Jyotirao Phule, Ambedkar, as well as the Black Panthers Movement (an organisation that fought for African-American rights). Dalit Panthers have transfigured Marathi literature. In the Southern part of the country, writer-activists like Bama (Tamil Nadu) were bringing up a change. Bama was a Dalit feminist who delineated an autobiography titled Karukku (1992). The book explores the joys and sorrows in the lives of Dalit Christian women of Tamil Nadu. Omprakash Valmiki's autobiography Joothan (1997), is a strong piece that movingly talks about caste-based discrimination in Uttar Pradesh.

The literary world has witnessed the dawn of new Dalit writers who have transformed the space with their powerful writings. P. Sivakami is one of the most prominent Dalit writers of the present age. Her book The Grip of Change (2006) is an influential piece of writing, considered as one of the finest. VijilaChirrappad, a Dalit woman writer from Kerala, has published three collections to date. Her writings exhibit problems in the lives of women. Dev Kumar, born in 1972, is a Dalit writer as well as a dramatist who founded a theatre group (Apna Theatre) in 1992 and has produced several plays arousing Dalit consciousness. Meena Kandasamy is one of the most famous feminist writers of our country and her writings are deeply linked to the anti-caste movement. Earlier, the literary sphere was dominated by Dalit characters that didn't have a very strong voice (for example, Lakshmi from Children of God) whereas, the present-day characters are penned down in a bold spectrum.

Massive improvement in Dalit literature came all across the nation after independence. Dalit voices in Marathi,

Gujrati, Telugu, and Tamil looked upon Ambedkar as their inspiration.

Bengali Dalit literature has a diverse notion. The first specified printed Dalit text takes us back to 1916. Dalit Literature in Bengali is influenced by Harichand Thakur, a leader of the Motua community, along with Ambedkar being a major inspiration. Sekhar Bandyopadhyay's 'The Namasudra Movement' (2005) and SumitSarkar's 'Writing Social History' (1997) edify in detail how caste consciousness and anti-caste movements were introduced in colonial Bengal under the leadership of the Motuas.

But the most prominent and organized Dalit literary movement began in Bengal as late as 1992 after ChuniKotal's suicide. The protests against the acts which provoked it culminated in the formation of the 'Bangla Dalit Sahitya Sanstha'; a magazine, 'ChaturthaDuniya', devoted entirely to the nourishment and circulation of Dalit writings, was also launched. 'ChaturthaDuniya' (literally meaning the fourth world), on one hand, implies the world of the fourth 'varna' of the caste system (Sudras), while, on another focal point, articulates the testimonials of living in a world within the third world. This magazine has witnessed the rise of several important Dalit writers, notably Manohar Mouli Biswas, JatinBala, Kapil Krishna Thakur, Kalyani Charal, and Manju Bala among many others. These writers have unchained themselves and according to Debayudh Chatterjee, the Dalits have earned access to the Brahmanical tools of knowledge and writing and carved out a niche for themselves by employing literature as a plausible mode of resistance. Translation has enabled the Bengali Dalit writers to attain international recognition. We can expect certainly at this hour that the day is not far when names like Manoranjan Byapari or

Nakul Mallik would be evoked alongside Sunil Gangopadhyay or Shirshendu Mukhopadhyay to define the parameters of post-independent Bengali Literature.

Dalit1 writings in Bengal have flourished since the 1970s and in the past ten years, writers from the Dalit community have given readers a new vent into their own lives, coming from marginal backgrounds.

The emergence of Manohar Mouli Biswas

Manohar Mouli Biswas has painted a larger-than-life picture of his childhood by delineating intricate details of not only his everyday life but also his dormant anger against the brutal societal hegemonic structure, erupting through his lines in Surviving In My World: Growing Up Dalit in Bengal.

The other 'world' within Indian society can be viewed through this paper through the autobiography of Manohar Mouli Biswas. This world of Biswas is the world, where people are encountering the evils of caste discrimination. It depicts the difference between the society we live in and the harsh societal perils that marginalize a certain community of our kin. It is a tragedy for the Bengali society to pay privilege to the upper castes and disregard the people who are the reason for the well-fed state of the upper caste people. Biswas has aptly portrayed his unfortunate experiences within a Bengali society where he was subjected to alienation and treated inhumanly.

This paper also sheds light on Biswas's travel from the margin to the centre against the oppressive hegemonic mechanism of power, caste, and tradition that intends to subdue the voice of the marginalized people under the monopoly of the ideology of mainstream Bengali 'bhodrolok'2 culture and society. It will serve as a reflection of our society where caste creates barriers within our hearts, our love, and ourselves. Biswas has depicted the experiences of the community and he has conveyed them through his autobiography. Dalits have prevailed to be the subject to oppression regardless of time and Manohar Mouli Biswas quite justly has mirrored his sufferings as a Dalit in his work, Surviving in My World.

The portrayal of their world through Surviving in My World

Surviving in My World: Growing up Dalit in Bengal exhibits the author's relentless sense of pain and anguish distressing his mind since his childhood, being born in a subaltern background. The "bhadralok" community within the society have exercised the act of subduing the voice of the "namasudra"3 community for ages and have relished their position as imperial rulers in command of Bengal. I have endeavored to depict the sufferings inflicted upon the "namasudra" community in the hands of their "bhadralok" rulers narrated through the mouthpiece of Biswas in his autobiography. The equation of power has always found the "namasudra" community as crucial in terms of electoral politics whereas, in terms of unity, the "bhadralok" community has always treated them as Marginals.

Surviving In My World: Growing Up Dalit In Bengal is an eye-opener for the society as it showcases Biswas's struggles within the very system we are living in and the text quite prominently questions the system, thus opting for a change for egalitarianism. By pointing out the phrase "My World", the author has drawn a sharp contrast between the normative world where the higher castes are a part and the world in which the "namasudras" are constantly living on the edge. Their life is all about surviving. To change the system in which the society runs, Biswas has opted for a change in the structure of the society where every human being must be given equal preference irrespective of background or caste. I have drawn out ample examples from Dalit writers in Bengal who speak about the same vision that Manohar Mouli Biswas has. Many non-Dalit writers have also opted for a change in the social order and liberating the people of the margins and not only bringing them to the Center but acknowledging them as equal to everyone else.

According to Biswas, any person subject to oppression may be called a Dalit, regardless of his/her caste. To him, oppression is evident within every caste and has many different methods of subduing the weaker people to establish the strong one's dominance. Biswas goes down the pages of India's history and shows us how people in power have always exercised the practice of oppressing the weaker mass to establish their dominance in terms of political and socio-economical means.

The occupations of the "dom"4 community as Biswas was accustomed to the culture and was also a part of it requires a mention as well. The "dom" community consists of people who have been forsaken by the governments for decades. Biswas mentioned that the chief occupation of the "dom" community was making bamboo baskets, yet they were labelled as criminals by several Bengali authors who belonged to the "bhadralok" society. This gives us a glimpse into the imagination of the "bhadralok" mass as they generalize the marginal people as thieves, robbers, and even murderers. My thesis is a reflection of Biswas's tormented state of mind, being grown up in a marginal community, fighting for survival, and going through the extremes to get established in society.

PORTRAYAL OF THE INHUMANE SHALLOWNESS

"Red flag has thirst for blood;/ A rose of revolt."– from Manohar Mouli Biswas's poem 'Sangram', translated by Jaydeep Sarangi by the name 'Warfare', portray the excruciating suffering of the author, through the spectrum of his community as a whole, which he anticipated as a new world within the subaltern world. The "red flag" is an emblem of revolt whereas the "thirst for blood" signifies the deep longing for revenge on the hegemonic autocracy by those who are marginalized from mainstream Bengali society. Biswas has time and again tried to take apart the socially destructive practice of casting aside the Dalits or marginal people by the people in power, who relish their practice of neglecting their kin, the Dalits of Bengal.

Originally the work Surviving in My World: Growing Up Dalit in Bengal was written by Manohar Mouli Biswas in Bengali and was published in 2013 with the title Amar Bhubane Ami BecheThaki, whereas the English translation of the text was presented in 2015 and carries a subtitle: Growing Up Dalit in Bengal. If compared to the thriving translations of Tamil and Marathi Dalit literature, no significant work has been done with Bengali Dalit writings. Surviving in My World: Growing Up Dalit in Bengal is the first Bengali Dalit autobiography translated into English. The translators, Angana Dutta and Jaydeep Sarangi speak briefly, in the preface, about the 'biggest challenges they faced while trying to 'recreate for an English-reading audience, the unfamiliar artefacts, sceneries, soundscapes, fragrances, dialects and emotions of life experienced in more than half-a-century-old Bengal' (Dutta, 2015, Sarangi, 2015, p. xxii). The act of translation presents a multi-layered act of interpretation. If autobiography is itself an interpretation of one's life, translation adds a second layer of interpretation and the final translated text is offered to the reader's interpretive skills.

Surviving in My World: Growing Up Dalit in Bengal is a poignant delineation of the life of Dalits in Bengal before and after the 1947 Partition. Fragments of memories from the author's childhood narrate the fate of the caste-ridden community of Namasudras, who live in a marginal small village in East Bengal. Designated by the 'babus'5 as 'pork-eating 'namas (Biswas, 9), Biswas's community was objectified as a lower untouchable caste and shunned by the upper-class, who would neither enter their neighbourhood 'nor think about sit and eat together with them' (Biswas, p. 10). Biswas envisions his father's hardships to sustain the livelihood of the family, as hunger haunted their lives; they were dependent on the river Kali for food. Biswas memorises the year when the rice fields were submerged underwater due to flood and the crops were destroyed by brackish water, 'Famine descended upon the people of kali and Chitra riverbanks... there was not a bit of rice in anyone's home. Almost everyone started spending their days in starvation' (Biswas, 24).

People had to adapt to this harsh environment to survive as they were left on their own, with no governmental intervention. Alike Prisnika, 'growing up like the water hyacinth and dying like it, uncared for' (Biswas, p. 48), Biswas himself had to make out his formulae of survival. The harsh nature in Bengal taught him his first lesson against passivity. He elaborates a period in his childhood passed with a strange passion for fishing. He used to observe the movement of fish for hours and tried to learn their habits. The society of fish, as Biswas mentions, was also governed by a distinct social hierarchy of aristocrats and non-aristocrats. Biswas could easily distinguish a category of fish, the 'chuno, puti, koi, magur fishes'

(Biswas, 72), which behaved like lower castes: "They were just happy to remain alive. The level of their demands was humble. They were joyful just to live. Their presence beside the aristocrats was completely unwanted, a mismatch. This is what I saw. I found profound similarities in the people of my community with those non-aristocrats." (Biswas, 72)

Biswas chose to walk against the wind and found the best means of the change in education during those long hours of observation. Manohar was a first-generation learner from his family as coming off a Dalit background, his predecessors could not imagine being educated within the malignant caste-obsessed society of Bengal where only children of the 'bhadralok' class could only get into schools; the rest were seen less humanely. The question of education opens his text. 'The children must get educated' (Biswas, 1) is his father's often repeated sentence, recollected with great pleasure. The first two sentences, exhibit a contrasting space with a thatched hut and mud veranda, juxtaposed with the father's inspiring words, implying the importance of education in changing people's lives. The story of getting the education and the adversities Biswas tackled in getting rudimentary school supplies to roam across the whole autobiography. This fascinating story of triumph acts as a poetic justice where a Dalit individual overthrows a diseased social system.

It is quite evident from Biswas's own experiences that there is a social hierarchy within the larger form of Hindu society. Although the people belong to the same religion, i.e., Hinduism, they are divided by the millennia-old malpractice of caste division. Unlike in many parts of the world where racial division played the most cynical role in fragmenting mankind, in India, the fragmentation is rooted deep inside the Hindu religion, which dictates the division of people according to their caste: Brahmins, Kshatriyas, Vysyas, and Sudras accordingly. The 'Sudras' have since the Brahmin-dominated ages, have been used by the upper castes of India for their well-being whereas the 'Sudras' themselves are treated in a much less humane way.

Biswas delineates excruciating episodes of suffering and torment, keeping away any form of pathos or self-victimization, he simply states, "Just as everyone is proud of their community, I am no exception" (Biswas, 57). The autobiography ends with the remembrance of a personal trauma related to his caste. The final episode where the mother of Rushita, the girl he used to love, described the impossibility of their marriage because he belonged to an untouchable caste, remains deeply encrusted in his memory: 'The words with which Rushita's mother had bade farewell remained alive as a deep wound time could not heal' (Biswas, p. 85). Recollecting these agonising memories enriches the autobiography with a testimonial quality crucial for any response to trauma. Though Biswas systematically utilized the word 'autobiography' in his book as well as in interviews, the translators added the proposal in their introduction using the term 'testimonial' to focus on the woes of a whole group or community of Dalit people. Beverley (2004: 41) provides a pertinent definition, 'Testimonio represents an affirmation of the individual subject, even of individual growth and transformation, but in connection with a group or class situation marked by marginalization, oppression, and struggle.'(Beverley, 2004:41)

Seen from this perspective, Surviving in My World offers a significant case of testimonial, documenting the life of Bengali Dalits. Indeed, Biswas pens down the stories of 'a community that remained neglected away from the watch of the nation's administration. The people born in nature lived in their way and even died in their way' (Biswas, p. 48). In India, Dalit autobiographies are in many ways, the oppositional resistant 'micro-narratives' that retrieve "the small voices of history" (Guha, 1996, 1-12). The narrative occasionally takes the form of 'witness' or 'testimonial literature' where the narrator both witnesses and takes part in the events of witnessing simultaneously. (Pal, Bidisha, and Md Mojibur Rahman, 2021).

. Unlike the Dalits of another part of the country, Dalits in Bengal are the victims of politics of exclusion in the meta-narratives of history and social discourse. Interrogating My Chandal Life: An Autobiography of a Dalit (2017) by Manoranjan Byapari also unfolds the very tendency while depicting the strikingly suppressed and alternative history of the marginalization of Bengal. Biswas, in the Introduction6, mentions that in their world there are people who "have no taste for narrations of pain" (Biswas, p.xix) and later on asserts in an interview with Jaydeep Sarangi, "a kind of psycho-pleasure works within me at this moment which has pushed me ahead to forget the melancholy of the past... The sadness had touched me severely once, and I want to forget it forever." (Sarangi) The shallowness of the Bengali society that compelled Manohar Mouli Biswas to create his world of suffering in Surviving in My World reflected through his words when he was interviewed by me.

In the interview of Biswas (given later in this paper), we can quite evidently observe his disappointment towards the Bengali society, of which he was an integral part. Although he grew up in a Dalit family, he was in some ways optimistic about the societal condition of Bengal which he hoped would become egalitarian but he gradually became frustrated and enraged when he witnessed the unchanged, malignant nature of the caste-obsessed face of the society he lived in. A shocking experience in the vicious caste-obsessed society was when he came to know about the heartbreaking news of the death of a Dalit girl named ChuniKotal, who was insulted by her teacher in front of her classmates and was compelled to commit suicide whereas the people responsible for her death did not receive any punishment from neither the justice system nor the government of Bengal at the time. This provoked Biswas and many other noteworthy marginal voices to raise protests against such inhumane practices. According to Biswas, a world within the world that is visible around us had become uncovered at this point of time. There was a visible barrier between the 'bhadralok' community and the "namasudra" community within the Bengali society.

According to Sankar Prasad Singha and Indranil Acharya in Survival and Other Stories: Bangla Dalit Fiction in Translation (2012), Marxists in India have always shied away from addressing the caste issues in public. For them, caste does not exist at all. Their rhetoric is all about class and class alone. This does not mean that the caste system does not exist in Bengal. Issues relating to caste discriminations have been addressed in the past by many well-known writers of Bengal, not to mention Bankimchandra Chatterjee and Rabindranath Tagore. Dalits in Bengal, as elsewhere in India, have been ostracized and neglected throughout these years by the caste society. The stories in the anthology expose how inhuman treatments are meted out to the Dalits by the upper castes.

CONCLUSION

In Manohar Mouli Biswas's poem "Phoolan" (translated by Jaydeep Sarangi), Biswas writes: "Oh! Phoolan, you have come from/ The lowest caste/ From a marginalised village." This further portrays Biswas's world of suffering, in which, the rebellious marginal woman named Phoolan Devi also dwelled. Biswas refers to the words "lowest caste" to portray the fragmented society in Bengal and also to specify the shallowness that has inundated Bengali society for ages. Biswas informs the oppressors to be aware that although the Dalits resist the oppression, they can still fight back like Phoolan13 and raise their voices. The feeling of "deprivation due to discrimination" is psychological and is not fully substantiated by the author in the text. In many ways, the "deprivation" is due to relentless nature, the remoteness of his land, the landscape he was born in. Surviving in My World by Manohar Mouli Biswas is the portrayal of a remote, natural landscape and life of a pre-Independence Dalit community. In this book, he narrates experiences such as raising paddy, fishing, purchasing pigs, rowing boats on shallow water, plucking fruits and flowers for food, mattress-weaving, and catching birds as unique experiences of his community. To the reader today, such descriptions appear fantastic and cause nostalgia in the writer as well. He writes: "This is the autobiography of remembering the bygone memories of my community." (Biswas, p. 78). Through these specifications, Biswas has illustrated their world, which is diverse from the world of the privileged Brahmanical society. Thereby, Surviving in My World: Growing Up Dalit in Bengal has specifically referred to the trundle of the Dalit trajectory to form a new world in Bengal.

Notes

1. The word Dalit, meaning "broken/scattered" in Sanskrit and Hindi, is a word used for those who have been

subjected to untouchability. Dalits were excluded from the four-fold varna system of Hinduism and were seen as forming a fifth varna, also known by the name of Panchama.

2. A Bengali term for the new class of 'gentlefolk' who emerged during British rule in India (approximately 1757 to 1947) in the Bengal region in the eastern part of the Indian subcontinent.
3. An Indian Avana community originating from certain regions of Bengal, India. The community was earlier known as*Chandala*or *Chandal*, a term usually considered a slur. They were traditionally engaged in cultivation and as boatmen. They lived outside the four-tier ritual varna system and thus were outcastes.
4. A lower caste community of the Hindu religion.
5. 'Babu' often referred to a native Indian clerk in British India. The word was originally used as a term of respect attached to a proper name, the equivalent of "mister", and "babuji" was used in many parts to mean "sir" as an address of a gentleman; their class lifestyle also called "babu culture". In some historical novels, it would be seen some gestures of that so-called culture. They have enjoyed a number of privileges for being the service holder of the British Raj. Even their social demands expressed much importance. The British officials treated them as near workers who have both Indian and British connections.
6. Introduction to Biswas's book Surviving in My World: Growing Up Dalit in Bengal.
7. Varna system is the social stratification based on the Varna, caste. Four basic categories are defined under this system - Brahmins (priests, teachers, intellectuals), Kshatriyas (warriors, kings, administrators), Vaishyas

(agriculturalists, traders, farmers) and Shudras (workers, labourers, artisans).

8. Chandal is a Sanskrit word for someone who deals with the disposal of corpses and is a Hindu lower caste, traditionally considered to be untouchable.
9. An ancient legal text among the many Dharmaśāstras of Hinduism. It was one of the first Sanskrit texts to have been translated into English in 1794, by Sir William Jones, and was used to formulate the Hindu law by the British colonial government. It presents itself as a discourse given by Manu (Svayambhuva) and Bhrigu on dharma topics such as duties, rights, laws, conduct, virtues and others. The text's fame spread outside India, long before the colonial era.
10. The word "Chatur" means four and Varna means 'Groups', means four groups. There were four groups of people Brahmins (Teachers), Kshatriya (Fighters), Vaishya (Traders) and Sudra (Producers).
11. "Prāṇāyāma" is the practice of breath control in yoga. In modern yoga as exercise, it consists of synchronising the breath with movements between asanas, but is also a distinct breathing exercise on its own, usually practised after asanas.
12. Phoolan Devi, popularly known as "Bandit Queen", was an Indian bandit and later a member of parliament. Born into a poor family in rural Uttar Pradesh, Phoolan endured poverty, child marriage and had an abusive marriage before taking to a life of crime.
13. A phoenix (/ˈfiːnɪ ks/; Ancient Greek: φοῖνιξ, phoînix) is a long-lived bird that cyclically regenerates or is otherwise born again. Associated with the sun, a phoenix obtains new life by arising from the ashes of its

predecessor according to Greek Folklore. Some legends say it dies in a show of flames and combustion, others that it simply dies and decomposes before bein

Works Cited

Primary Materials

Biswas, Manohar Mouli. *Surviving in My World: Growing Up Dalit in Bengal.* Trans. Sarangi, Jaydeep, Dutta, Angana. Kolkata: Stree Samya, 2015. Print.

Byapari, Manoranjan. *Interrogating My Chandal Life: An Autobiography of a Dalit.* Trans. Mukherjee, Sipra. Kolkata: Sage, Samya, 2017. Print.

Secondary Materials

Ben Driss, Hager. Book Review: Manohar Mouli Biswas, *Surviving in My World: Growing Up Dalit in Bengal*

Byapari, Manoranjan, Mukherjee, Meenakshi, *Economic and Political Weekly* Vol. 42, No. 41 (Oct. 13 - 19, 2007)

Byapari, Manoranjan. Is There Dalit Writing In Bangla? (https://www.jstor.org/stable/40276544?seq=1) (Accessed on 25th March 2020)

Chatterjee, Debayudh. "A Brief Introductory Overview of Bengali Dalit Literature" (https://blog.ilfsamanvay.org/2016/03/22/a-brief-introductory-overview-of-bengali-dalit-literature/) (Accessed on 31st March 2020)

Essay on Dalit Literature (https://www.ukessays.com/essays/english-literature/the-term-dalit-literature-english-literature-essay.php) (Accessed on 26th March 2020)

Pal, Bidisha, and Md Mojibur Rahman. "DALIT AUTOBIOGRAPHY AS AUTOETHNOGRAPHY: A STUDY OF MANOHAR MOULI BISWAS'SURVIVING IN MY WORLD." REVISTA DE ETNOGRAFIE SI FOLCLOR-JOURNAL OF ETHNOGRAPHY AND FOLKLORE 1-2

(2021): 5-19.

Sarangi, Jaydeep. Book Review: Manohar Mouli Biswas, *Surviving in My World: Growing Up Dalit in Bengal*(https://www.academia.edu/33037557/Review_M_M_Biswas_Surviving_in_My_World.pdf) (Accessed on: 21st March 2020)

Singha, Sankar Prasad, Acharya, Indranil. *Survival And Other Stories*: *Bangla Dalit Fiction in Translation*. New Delhi: Orient Blackswan, 2012.

CHAPTER XIII

THE TRAUMA OF ISOLATION: A CRITICAL DISCOURSE ON SYLVIA PLATH'S POETRY

Parvathi

Ph. D. Research Scholar

Department of English, Muslim Arts College,

Thiruvithancode, Tamilnadu.

ABSTRACT

This paper examines the poetry of Silvia Plath to identify a new perspective on trauma and isolation that itself functions as the narrative voice in her poetry. To explore how traumatic experiences are presented; this paper takes a close look on the selected poems of Plath's with the present traumatic experiences as well as to connect the audience. It also constitutes how women were isolated and treated in the social scene. One such poetess who suffered a dreadful isolation by the prominent male personalities of her life is Sylvia Plath. She directly infused her anger towards men in two of her poems "Daddy" and "Lady Lazarus". So this paper mainly focuses on some select poems of Plath and brings out the isolation, trauma, depression and psychological suffering faced by women due to suppression.

Keywords: Trauma, Depression, Isolation, Suppression and Psychology.

• • •

The trauma of Isolation: A Critical Discourse on Sylvia Plath's PoetryTrauma of Isolation: A Critical Discourse on Sylvia Plath's Poetry

Introduction

Sylvia Plath a well renowned American poet born on 27th October 1932, at Boston, Massachusetts, U.S and has a shorter span of life. She leads a pathetic life for nearly thirty years and committed suicide on February 11,1963. She was graduated from Smith College and her first collection of poems titled as 'The Colossus'. As she was psychologically disturbed most of her works contain the theme of alienation, self- destruction and death. The vision embodied in the poetry of Sylvia Plath is complex, prismatic and tantalizing, as it springs from one of the most enigmatic personalities of American literature with complex personality and multi-layered consciousness. Plath's short but eventful life has a hotbed of controversies. Her poems usually have a touch of the Holocaust and were painted gothic. She got married and began her life with Ted Hughes in 1956. She doesn't have a happy life even then. Ted Hughes had an affair with another girl Assia Wevill, and the couple got separated in 1962. Then she went into depression, tried to kill her own self and that pushed her to be under psychiatric hospitalization. During her last five years she wrote some of her famous poems "Daddy" and "Lady Lazarus". Some of her notable works were "The Bell Jar", "Ariel", "Johnny Panic" and "The Bible of Dreams". She was awarded the Pulitzer Prize posthumously in 1982. She was acclaimed to be one of the prominent writers during her period. In the New York Times book review, Joyce Carol Oates described Plath as "one of the most celebrated and controversial of post-war poets writing in English".

Daddy

"Daddy" was written on October 12, 1962, four months before her death and one month after her separation from Ted Hughes. The poem employs controversial metaphors of the Holocaust to explain Plath's complex relationship with her father, Otto Plath, who died shortly after her eighth birthday. The poem is embellished with dark and painful allegory which gives the exact picture of her sufferings. The poem mostly contains surreal imagery and allusion with dark cinematic language.

"The vampire who said he was you
And drank my blood for a year,
Seven years if you want to know."
(Sylvia Plath, Daddy)

Lady Lazarus

Lady Lazarus is written during her final days in 1962, originally included in Ariel which was published in 1965, two years after her death by suicide. It is considered to be one of Plath's best poems and has a subject of plethora of literary criticism since its publication. It is commonly interpreted as an expression of Plath's suicidal attempts and thoughts. This poem depicts her thoughts about suicide as she breaks her marital bond with Ted Hughes. Her hatred towards the whole male gender was described perfectly in this poem. This poem also tries to paint the dark and gothic effects of holocaust as her sufferings were compared to the Holocaust victims. She also used mythological creatures to give more terror in the poem. The poem is filled with more punctuation which literally describes her emotion towards death, society and men.

"Dying
Is an art, like everything else.
I do it exceptionally well.
(Sylvia Plath, Lady Lazarus)

Theme of Isolation

Both Plath's father and her husband left her alone in life and that serves as a main reason for her hatred towards all men. Even though they suppressed her but that seems to be secondary rather the primary reason was they were not available when she needed the most. Even after the death of her father, Plath explores his undead influence on her life by bringing in another man as her husband. The speaker clearly connects her father's effect on her life with her husband as he was a "model" of him. Both men in the poem makes harmful effects on the speaker.

In Lady Lazarus also, she says that she was already in depression which made her to commit suicide but once she got recovered from the death, the people sees her like a miracle and started to cook up stories about her suicide. For them her suicide is nothing serious but a time pass matter to crunch like a peanut. These situations pushed her into depression and thus result in neurosis and trauma. As a result of this she hated her life and thus made to attempt suicide often.

Trauma theory on Plath's poem.

As Plath's poems are highly embellished with pain and depression they can be analyzed on the basis of Freud's psychoanalysis theory. Plath didn't get a happy father-daughter relationship so she expects that she might get a happy relationship at least with her husband. But unfortunately Ted Hughes, her husband also betrays her by having relationship with another woman. As she was not prepared to face this situation, it ended up in fear which combined with the reactions of the people around her pushed her into depression and thus resulted in neurosis. Also Freud says people who were marked with traumatic neurosis has "compulsion to repeat" the memory of the painful event with the hopes of mastering the unpleasant feelings(Freud 1920:19). As she used to repeat her painful memories caused by her father and husband even after so many years justifies that she is affected with traumatic neurosis.

Furthermore, the effects of repression prove that she is neurotic. Because Freud in his theory says that the repressed feeling will be somehow stored in the subconscious memory. He says, the fundamental "phenomenon of hysteria" involves dissociation which the authors argue is a defence mechanism that arises from repression. As Plath didn't get her father's love and care during her childhood times her feelings were repressed also her husband's betrayal made her to hate the whole male gender, which resulted in the revenging attitude. She literally wished to kill men. But unfortunately she was unable to do that in her real life she achieves it through her poems for mental satisfaction.

Also one of the concerns for the emergence of Trauma theory is to create awareness for the psychic scars caused by Holocaust. Plath's poem contains much imagery that represents Holocaust and Second World War. Through her usage of gothic words to explain with these imageries it is clear that she is also psychologically affected by the terrors of Holocaust. This also serves as a major reason for her depression which forced her to a stage that she compares herself with the Holocaust victims and imagined as if she is dying in the same way and she admits that she loves doing it. Such things clearly portray how psychic she is.

Conclusion

Being in depression is normal for a person but being in a state of depression which resulted in so much obsession about suicide is something abnormal. Plath is such kind of a personality. How to commit suicide and how to self-harm in different ways seems to be her all-time job and she says she loves doing it and also feels that she is so much tired of doing it. The main reason for this situation is isolation, longing for love and betrayal which pushed a woman to this state of trauma. If she was able to portray the gothic effects in such a lively manner, then how intense her scars would be. Women are somehow getting disturbed by men despite years.

Works Cited

1. https://www.poetryfoundation.org/poets/sylvia-plath

2. https://www.britannica.com/biography/Sylvia-Plath

3. https://www.britannica.com/topic/Daddy-poem-by-Plath#ref1113290

4. https://owlcation.com/humanities/Analysis-of-Poem-Daddy-by-Sylvia-Plath

5. https://owlcation.com/humanities/Analysis-of-Poem-Lady-Lazarus-by-Sylvia-Plath

6. https://en.m.wikipedia.org/wiki/Psychological_trauma

7. https://www.oxfordbibliographies.com/view/document/obo-9780199791286/obo 9780199791286-0147.xml

8. https://www.quora.com/What-is-trauma-theory-in-English-literature

9. https://www.google.com/amp/s/literariness.org/2017/06/21/sigmund-freud-and-the trauma-theory/amp/.

CHAPTER XIV

ANALYSIS ON ROLE OF SOCIETY IN IDENTITY CRISIS OF TRANSGENDERS

Liji Rose Thomas

ABSTRACT

Gender is the word that is defined as one's identity as female or male or as entirely male. Where Trans is defined as a person whose sense of personal identity and gender does not correspond with their sex. In that sense, Transgender, a biological and social minority or as a belief, indicate the identity crisis and contrast of practices that demonstrated between or beyond the classification of male or female. Transgender people have a gender identity or gender expression that differs from their sex assigned at birth. The trans community is incredibly diverse. Social attitudes to transgender persons and other gender minorities vary around the world, and in many traditions, preconception and social stigma are common. Society even in this 21st century still does not understand who is trans? What is trans? What are types of trans? Society is still in a stereotype belief that there are only two kinds of categories Men and Women. Our society has a set of ideas about gender. This results in a tension of identity crisis that adversely affects the physical and mental status of trans people that categorized as (LGBTQIA) straight, bisexual, lesbian, gay, asexual, pansexual, queer etc. This paper discusses and analyzes the social attitude towards transgenders and the identity crisis they face during a lifetime.

Keywords: Gender, Trans and LGBTQIA community.

• • •

Analysis on Role of Society in Identity Crisis of Transgenders

"... it is fatal for anyone who writes to think of their sex. It is fatal to be a man or woman pure and simple; one must be woman-manly or man-womanly. It is fatal for a woman to lay the least stress on any grievance; to plead even with justice any cause; in any way to speak consciously as a woman. And fatal is no figure of speech; for anything is written with that conscious bias is doomed to death. It ceases to be fertilized. Brilliant and effective, powerful and masterly, as it may appear for a day or two, it must wither at nightfall; it cannot grow in the minds of others. Some collaboration has to take place in the mind between the woman and the man before the act of creation can be accomplished. Some marriage of opposites has to be consummated. The whole of the mind must lie wide open if we are to get the sense that the writer is communicating his experience with perfect fullness."

— Virginia Woolf, *A Room of One's Own*

Gender identity is the personal sense of one's own gender. Culture determines gender roles and what is masculine and feminine. Gender identity is defined as a personal conception of oneself as male or female (or rarely, both or neither). An identity crisis is a developmental event that involves a person questioning their sense of self or place in the world. This concept is intimately related to the concept of gender role, which is defined as the outward manifestations of personality that reflect gender identity.

We're born our gender identity is no secret. We're either a boy or a girl. From here we should start thinking about the other side of gender identity. Other than a firm belief of being men or women there's a group of people around as who born different.

Transgender people have a gender identity or gender expression that differs from the sex that they were assigned at birth. If one's gender identity matches the gender assigned at birth, this is called cis-gender. But, if a sense of unease or dissatisfaction that a person may have because of a contradiction between their biological sex and their gender identity. Jack Drescher, a New York psychiatrist who was a part of the American Psychiatric Association's workgroup on gender identity, revised the latest manual on mental disorders, the (Diagnostic and Statistical Manual Disorders) DSM-5. He says, usually, with a mental disorder, we try and change the person's mind. "This is the only mental disorder where the treatment is changing the body. In a typical mental disorder, we try to make those symptoms go away. Drescher says, 'It's not called a disorder, but it is in the handbook of mental disorders. "Nowadays, we are assigning gender even before birth. We have become socially conditioned to participate in the gendering of children at the earliest possible moment—whenever a sonogram can identify its genitalia. Gender-reveal parties have become a trendy way to celebrate the child's fate, steering them down a life of masculine or feminine ideals before ever meeting them" (George Matthew Johnson,12)

Objectives of the Study

The primary objective of the investigation is to study the issues related to the identity crisis of transgender

i. To study the socio-economic and educational background of transgender.

ii. To study the problem faced by transgender in their day to day life.

iii. To study the welfare programs running by the government for the welfare of transgender and their weaknesses.

iv. To study how transgender uplift their status and social acceptance in society.

Gender Dysphoria

Gender identity typically develops in stages: Childhood, Teenage, Youth. Children if experience serious distress that results from an incongruence between one's sex assigned at birth and one's gender identity it is called "Gender Dysphoria". A child's gender identity isn't always indicative of one particular gender expression, the expression and behaviours might be bathroom behaviour, selection of toys, selection of dress etc. Make sure the family gives time to the child to tell what they feel. Unfortunately, transgender teens receive near-constant reminders that their body and mind are not in sync, when they are not allowed to transition, they may suffer from depression, anxiety and an increased risk of inflicting self-harm. Although a possibility of discrimination occurs in school also. Sexual minority status is a key risk factor for suicide among lesbian, gay, bisexual youth; however, it has not been studied among transgender youth. Transgender youth are usually dependent on their parents for care, shelter, financial support, and other needs transgender youth face different challenges compared to adults.

Unfortunately, transgender youth still experience high levels of harassment, bullying, discrimination and even family rejection. When parents and families of transgender youth talk openly about those concerns, it can provide support to those who are still struggling with their own fears. The phenomenon of people who identify as another gender is a relatively new concept in the scientific world and an even newer concept to society. The word 'transgender' did not appear until the publication of Harry Benjamin's seminal publication, The Transsexual Phenomenon. In his 1966 work, Benjamin creates three categories; those who "merely want to 'dress', go out 'dressed', and to be accepted as women," those who find themselves in a "more severe stage of an emotional disturbance," and those who are fully transexual.

In describing transsexuality, Benjamin notes the alienation from society that transgendered people experience. The transgender community has been listed as a criminal tribe since a century ago during the British empire and since then has been misunderstood, ostracized, marginalized and discriminated against till today. The ignorance has driven out many transgenders from home and families and till today, many transgenders have remained beggars seeking rights and have been exploited sexually. Though trans are considered the worst people a huge number of socially respected people utilize them sexually because they are now even an oppressed community. Why did all Trans people consider sex workers by society? Is that true? Why are trans people not getting educated? Why trans not doing job in medical fields, IT area, or in any corporate companies explains? What explains public opinion towards transgender people, rights, and candidates? Through this chapter, we discuss and explains attitudes regarding:

(i) the personal characteristics of transgender people
(ii) a variety of transgender rights; and

(iii) transgender candidates for public office.

Lack of knowledge in Law, Transgenders are being badly attacked by society. The Transgender Persons (Protection of Rights) Act, 2019 ('Transgender Persons Act') seeks to recognize the identity of transgender persons and prohibit discrimination in, inter alia, the fields of education, employment, healthcare, holding or disposing of property, holding public or private office and access to and Society has failed to accept transgender's gender identity due to which they have suffered from discrimination, social oppression and physical violence. Compared to other countries Trans people face challenges in India, the main problems that are being faced by the transgender community area of discrimination from employment, educational facilities, habitat, lack of medical facilities: like HIV and hygiene, depression, hormone pill abuse, tobacco and alcohol abuse, and problems related to marriage and adoption.

Misinterpretation about the term 'transgender'

Transgender is not an expression restricted to persons whose pudenda are intermixed but it is a cover term of people whose gender expression, identity or behaviour differs from the norms expected from their birth sex. Various transgender identities fall under this category including transgender male, (MTF) and female to male (FTM). It also includes cross-dressers

(Those who wear clothes of the other), genderqueer people (they feel they belonged to either both genders or neither gender) and transsexuals.

Abuse affects the Transgender Community

One of the most fundamental principles of being in a relationship is to love and accept someone for who they are. Now, we don't mean accepting unhealthy tendencies, like a quick temper and being overly critical, but more the unique things that make someone special. Woefully, our society not usually shows acceptancy and kindness towards the things that make someone special, especially when it comes to people who don't obey conventional gender identities. Sometimes it's prime to show love to someone specifically anyone who identifies as transgender, is to love them for the betterment of their life and it's vital. We at one cherish and accept that everybody merits a sound relationship and know that each individual took a place in our development for later. And whereas the subtleties of a relationship can contrast depending on how you identify marginalized communities may confront particular challenges. Here we discuss the several cases of abuse from a society that affects the identity reveal of the transgender community:

(1) Relationship abuse

(2) They confront separation and battle to be accepted

(3) Their identity and sexuality can be utilized against them

(4) Solid relationship models are hard to find for Trans

(5) Obscured gender identity may make it harder to recognize mishandle

(6) Limited resources to help Trans people

(7) Higher Suicide Rate

Domestic abuse also called "domestic violence "or "intimate partner violence", can be defined as a pattern of behaviour in any relationship but to trans people, the risk factor is high. 30%-50% of trans communities experience dating violence compared to 20%-33% of the general population. Transgenders who face rejection from family and loved ones after revealing their identity are put through badgering and oppression. Trans people may face an identity crisis in personal life mainly because partners may try to abuse them using their identity by shaming them, and making them feel inferior or making them feel they are born to be abused. Insulting verbally, by making a thought imposed on their mind that they are not good for anything, or they'll not be accepted or loved by anyone and all these thoughts leads to strong insecurity feel for trans people.

Society shows high interest in playing on trans insecurity and sexual abuse as they don't have a strong partner Lack of healthy relationships of trans people with the society leads to all physical and mental harassment. Often the legal system is against them, police and authorities show less interest in helping transgenders if they may abuse or harassed by the public or shows more eagerness to be convicted. Government authority's refuse to give valid documents for homeless transgenders for receiving government benefits as a citizen. All these practices should be changed because in this 21st-century globalized world human and rational change is inevitable

How Society can support Transgenders?

- Educate ourselves about transgender issues. Allow trans-related in our book collection, make kids read from childhood, attend conferences etc.
- Make a good behavioural attitude towards people with a gender identity crisis.
- Support the right for trans people membership in various sociocultural identity groups (race, social class, disability, age, religion etc.)
- Avoid unwanted classification to maintain gender discrimination, and allow their names to be put as their identity.
- Make no conclusions about the sexual orientation of transgender people.

- Gender nonconformity is not synonymous with transgender identity. Not everyone who appears androgynous or who identifies as transgender or wants gender affirmation treatment is transgender.
- Cleanse your mind to welcome transgenders in your friend circle, and help them.
- Ensure all legal supports for trans people around us. Educate people around us about the rights of the trans community from our knowledge.
- Familiarize ourselves with provincial laws, local and state laws that protect trans people from harassment and discrimination.

The UN Member States have unequivocally agreed to this new common agenda for the immediate future. The SDGs demand an unambiguous, farsighted, and inclusive demonstration of political will. Their language clearly reflects the most urgent needs of trans people, for whom freedom from violence and discrimination, the right to health and legal gender recognition are inextricably linked. Specifically, in regard to trans people, the SDGs are a call to immediate action on several fronts: governments need to engage with trans people to understand their concerns, unequivocally support the right of trans people to legal gender recognition, support the documentation of human rights violations against them, provide efficient and accountable processes whereby violations can be safely reported and action taken, guarantee the prevention of such violations, and ensure that the whole gamut of robust health and HIV services are made available to trans people. Only then can trans people begin to imagine a world that respects their core personhood, and a world in which dignity, equality, and wellbeing become realities in their lives.

The major findings and discussions of the study focused on the attempts made by the transgender for improving their image in society by requesting government jobs so that they contribute to social services. So, the government should think seriously about the welfare of trans people in any aspect. Let society never be a reason for the destruction for transgenders, and for making identity crisis, whereas society should stand for the uplifting trans community.

Systemic strategies to reduce the violence against trans people need to occur at multiple levels, including making perpetrators accountable, facilitating legal and policy reform that removes criminality, and general advocacy to sensitize the ill-informed about trans issues and concerns. Strengthening the capacity of trans collectives and organizations to claim their rights can also act as a counter to the impunity of violence. When trans people are provided legal aid and access to judicial processes, accountability can be enforced against perpetrators. Sensitizing the police to make them partners in this work can be crucial. When the political will is absent to support such attempts in highly adverse settings, trans organizations and allies can consider using international human rights mechanisms, such as shadow reports made to UN human rights processes like the Universal Periodic Review, to bring focus to issues of anti-trans violence and other human rights violations against trans people.

Providing equal access to housing, education, public facilities and employment opportunities, and developing and implementing anti-discrimination laws and policies that protect trans people in these contexts, including guaranteeing their safety and security, are essential to ensure that trans individuals are treated as equal human beings.

Works Cited

Elizabeth plumtree." How Gender Dysphoria Is Diagnosed,29,2021

v.Shaharban.Dr, IDENTITY CRISIS AND SOCIAL EXCLUSION-A STUDY ON TRANSGENDERS,2019.

Mrinalini S, TRANSGENDER IN SOCIETY Challenges and Solutions,2019

Faces of Cedars-Sinai, Dr, Maurice Garcia, Transgender Surgeon,2019

Ajay Amitabh Suman@ *AjayAmitabhSumanSpeaks,* MAR 30,2021

DSM-5 ®and Family Solutions Systems

Jessica Russo, PhD, J. Kelly Coker, PhD, Jason H. King, PhD-Psychology-201

Ajay Majumder, Rabin Tarafder, A Scientific Aspects of Transgenders, 201

My Story by Ms. Kalki, Founder/Directo

: http://www.sahodar.org, Email: aurokalki@gmail.

http://news.naij.com/64488.htm

https://www,loc.gov

http://www.bing.com/transgender+identity+cisis

http://cram.com/What-is-Transgender

CHAPTER XV

ANALYSING COVID 19 PANDEMIC AND ITS IMPACTS THROUGH THE TEXT LOCKDOWN LIAISONS.

Meera Sunny
M A English

ABSTRACT

Lockdown Liaisons is the first work to be written during India's first Lockdown period. It had initially published through the online platform into different parts. Later, once the lockdown got lifted it had published into the print format as a book with twenty-four chapters written in the form of short stories. Each chapter is the story of different people and how they dealt with the lockdown and the pandemic. This work also brings our attention to the various impacts in the Indian society or country.

INTRODUCTION

Covid19 has emerged as a global health threat to us. The devastating reaction of this pandemic has created a negative outlook among the people. The fear of death had developed among the minds of people. Thus, it had made a negative outlook towards the pandemic. The WHO Mentioned Covid 19 as the largest outbreak that the Modern World had ever seen. The arrival of Coronavirus had made our daily lives and communication into a limited space. It had taken over our lives by restricting us.

World Health Organization identified this disease on 31 December 2019 in Wuhan-China. The common symptoms of Covid-19 include fever, dry cough, and fatigue. When this disease started spreading in India, the lockdown was insisted by our Prime Minister on 24 March 2020 evening for 21 days to avoid the spread of the disease. Later after seeing the wide spreading of this disease, the lockdown was extended up to May and got relaxed from June. But still, Schools and Colleges got closed. People who were engaged in business like hotels, Cabs, Agriculture, Industry, etc. Covid had created a rapid transition in the mode of the education system also.

The term 'lockdown' can be viewed in the pandemic as a state of isolation or restricted access. It is a word used, advising individuals to stay at home or a sheltered place so that they are kept safe against the virus. 'Lockdown' is described as the imposition of stringent restrictions on travel, social interaction, and access to public spaces. In addition, Collins has announced that the word 'lockdown' had been declared as the word of the year as it encapsulates the shared experience of billions of people.

While checking the first phase of Lockdown that happened due to the contagious nature of the Corona Virus; People are made to sit in their living rooms and it made them restricted to the luxury of going outside. People started to engage more in online activities as there were no other modes to communicate with others and have entertainment as they used to enjoy before the Pandemic Strikes. Then, they started to accumulate lots of data feeds related to the virus and its causalities. The constant increase in the mortality rate had made the people into a panic-stricken behaviour. Through the various characters in this text and their dimensions, we can understand the varied complexities associated with the virus and how they dealt with the situation.

Social isolation and loneliness had affected the mental health of the people. Duration of quarantine, fear of infection, the fear of unemployment and work from home patterns, etc. had impacted extra stress to the individuals. We can also see the lack of basic supply of needs, situations where people are stuck at work locations, travel bans, closure of schools, and loss of their dear ones. And gradually, this breaks down the Mental Health of the people. A lot of workers had died due to the lockdown as they had to face accidents, starvation, police brutality, and denial of timely medical cases throughout this time. Covid 19 had brought our Meeting platforms and Classroom teachings into Online form. Apps like Zoom, Google Meet, Microsoft Teams, etc. become the Platforms for these things. People started to become more conscious of their hygiene and public hygiene too. Some people started doubting everything around them as they start to connect every matter related to the Virus.

LOCKDOWN LIAISONS

Literature has always impacted human thoughts and actions. Therefore, a sense of meaning and the need for existence can be identified in the people, and for that, they choose different choices and one of the powerful tools in that is literature that had been written during the times of crisis. Shobhaa De in her Work *Lockdown Liaisons* brings her glance at the problems that the world faces during the pandemic, especially in India. She writes how the people had gone- through the days of Lockdown and Chaos, blame, stigmatization, loneliness, depression, fear of the spread of the virus associated with it. The terms such as Social-distancing, Quarantine, sanitisers gained popularity among the mass during this period.

This workis a collection of short stories from the varied perspectives of men and women, rich and poor, young and old, brave and cowardly, cheerful and debilitated. This work ranges from the stories of "In Malibu Mansions to Open Letter to a Microbe" which is of twenty-four chapters. Author, Shobhaa De had chronicled her thoughts and deeds in her twenty- four chapters in the book.

The first chapter, "In Malibu Mansions" tells the story of a married couple Sajid and Rehana. Shuklaji is the oldest resident in that flat they lived and he does every job there without being properly paid. Sara was a food influencer and the gym partner of Rehana. As there were no restaurants opened Sara couldn't do any food reviews or blogs and this made her job title into nothing and no use. Gradually, she loses hope in the purpose of her life and she committed suicide. Here, the husband of the narrator always irritates her after losing her job due to the outbreak of the virus. The true depictions and unemployment are portrayed here through the characters and how they have been affected by it.

In the following second Chapter titled "Leaving," we can see the issues of Migrant Workers being discussed through the characters in it. The workers had been ill-treated and considered as the carriers for spreading the virus as they leave in unhealthy conditions. They had to travel on foot for a long distance which we had read in newspapers and seen on television. In chapter third, "After this Dubai" again we can see a married couple and how their relationship became weak with time being together. Here, we can see how the condition of the glam industry of tele-field is being broken or stuck through the job title carried by the narrator as a television scriptwriter. She had to pay back the hefty loans which she had taken and there was no source for her as no projects were going by her.

In chapter fourth titled, "Little Joyful Things" we can see the issues of a woman who lacks her identity and interests because of her husband and he treats her like a sex doll that is made up for only pleasure. We can see the plight of women who are being stuck alone in the houses during these times and had to serve more according to the purposes of men. In chapter five" Rasam and Weed" we can see two research scholar students who are being in love. The narrator takes her girlfriend to his home and they had adjusted with the parents. We can see the sister of the narrator warning him because his girlfriend had sneezed due to the smell of rasam and the sister thinks it is the symptom of the Corona.

In the sixth Chapter, "No Love No Lost" we can see an old television actress and her ungroomed face, body, and hair as there were no beauty clinics and her beauty assistant was there due to the Lockdown. She gets frustrated with her neighbours who don't take care of the Covid protocols seriously; which means the ones who don't wear masks properly and maintain social distancing. Because she is an aged woman and people like her will get affected soon and if anyone tested positive in the flat people will start to hate them as the municipal members will mark the flat and it will defame the reputation of her place.

In the seventh chapter," My Girlfriend's Theplas" we can see a Social worker girl who is helping the needy people around her with food and the people who need mental support by calling them and listening to their problems. Arati is the name of the character here and she is an actual example for a real-life Philanthropist such as Sonu Sood who had immensely worked hard for the welfare of the needy in those tough times of the Lockdown period.

In chapter eight," Angie's Benarsi Saree" we can see a handloom weaver and her family. During the festival of Eid where the family of the narrator had don't even bring new clothes and they had to sit the whole time at the home itself which indicates that how pandemic and lockdown had taken off the most precious moments in the people's lives and how they been under starvation, poverty. The narrator becomes lost as she hadn't get her money for the works she had done and most of her orders got cancelled due to the Lockdown.

In chapter nine, 'Vodka ... And Tonic" we can see the events of Zoom party hosting's, workloads, depressed state of minds The sleeping patterns of the people had changed in people due to the work from home schedules and also the lockdown which had made the people's mental state down. The inaccessibility of alcohol and how much people thrive for it as a medicine, etc. are being showcased through the situations in the life of Vicky and Manju who are characters in the story that we can find in our society also. The physical abuses Manju had to face is also mentioned here as it was one of the very strong problem women faced during this time as couples spend most of the time together.

In chapter ten titled, 'Stuck" we can see the narrator who is an employer is being stuck at his workplace. Here, we can see he is escaping from his troublemaking illicit girlfriend by making her convinced by the help of others that he is having the symptoms of the virus and by the fear of being tested as positive and the after all effects she needs to face as everyone will isolate the one who is infected she runs away. Here, we can see how much scary image the virus had made among the people.

In chapter eleven "Doctor, Doctor" we can see the working conditions of doctors at the Pandemic time. Even it was a Lockdown period they need to go to work. They had to wear the PPE Suits, gloves, and extra masks through the work and it is not an easy thing to sit in the PPE kit for long hours. It was a huge task for them to get out of it for even to pee. Sitting inside a PPE suit is like a boiled lobster and the doctors had to face this throughout. This chapter discusses the conditions through which a doctor goes through at the duty ward by analysing the characters in it.

Next in chapter twelve, "Peace at Last" we can see the domestic and sexual assaults within the marriage again a repeated thing in the stories of this text. When everyone got stuck at their home for some category of men think sex as a thing with which they can indulge for passing time. But they even didn't care about the side of their partner. Women are working way harder to make their family comfortable and without consent of her most of the time they got tortured in the name of conjugal rights.

In chapter thirteen, "Wedding Cancelled" we can see the arrangements for a huge wedding that is being cancelled. The bride feels devasted as all her plans and the dreams for her big day had collapsed. She had spent a hefty amount as money for the designer outfits for her and fiancé and all that became in vain as they couldn't conduct the wedding and even no refunds or discounts will be issued for these dresses. Later her fiancé also had started to avoid her as his restaurant business which he started using the borrowed money had to shut according to the instructions by the government for Lockdown. Here we can see how a lot of people's dreams and projects got shattered due to Corona Virus.

In chapter fourteen titled "A Pressure Cooker Romance," we can see a girl who once feels annoyed by the whistling of the pressure cooker slowly started to enjoy it. Because the only thing she was accumulated during the lockdown was her neighbour's pressure cooker whistle. This indicates the emptiness of the surroundings which once was overpowered with noises had now become silent by the absence of people, busy crowds, stray dogs, etc.

In chapter fifteen "From Pomegranates to Love Letters," the issue of depression is again being addressed through the female character as she feels lonely and broke due to her relationship which made her no access to her beloved even to convince him what happened between or to cherish back the memories again in real. The closure of roads and travels bans are also discussed through the narrator our female protagonist as she wants to meet her lover and he is out of town and had blocked her from everything after posting a memory of them publicly on social media. As everyone does she spent her time in lockdown by checking and recollecting the old photos and by journaling her feelings towards her lover by hoping and writing letters which she thinks can be handed over once the lockdown gets lifted.

In chapter sixteen titled, "No Chicken Please" we can see a high-class old lady who decides to stay at her maid's home because there was no one to look her in the flat at the time of the pandemic and no outsiders were even not allowed entry in the flat. The old lady tried to adjust to the foods made at her maid's home and facilities thereby drinking and having the same foods as her maid and using the common Indian toilet. The lack of health care workers can also be seen here. Because most of them return to their native land due to the fear of the unprotected surroundings they need to work and the deadly nature of the disease as gets spread fast.

In chapter seventeen, "Beach House Birthday" we can see a celebrity (film actor) who is being stuck at his beach house after his birthday party. He started to feel irritated with his wife and her friends. And he is also telling them about the current situation of the film industry with new works and producers or directors calling for the date because they even. Start to fall into debt as there were no theatres to showcase their art or work. At first, people look forward to what the celebrities do and how they spend their time during lockdown by checking their social media feeds. And later they also get borrowed of it and don't care about it. These things indicate the lockdown trends that went on the social media during the lockdown period; like cooking and baking videos, dalgona coffee, workout posts, etc.

In chapter eighteen, "The Man Who Wanted More" the sexual and domestic violence towards a woman by her husband and his family in the name of dowry is shown. The husband is trying to rape her for denying his conjugal rights and always irritates her mental health by saying bad words about her family and her. This indicates how much women at the lockdown period had suffered from the husband's laws and husband in the form of verbal and physical abuses.

Next, in chapter nineteen, "Ganapati Bapa Morya" we can see a child named Ameya who is a strong devotee of Ganapati. And the child here is missing the old days where he used to visit the religious shrines of Ganapati and the rituals he attended and celebrated at the festival time of Ganapati. Ameya's father was a Municipal Member in Corporation and he tells the increased number of deaths day by day and there were no beds for patients in hospitals too. The dead bodies of Covid infected Patients are being electrically cremated. Ameya's mother who is a teacher had also expressed her worries along with her fellow teachers as the students are losing their years for the higher studies to the pandemic and lockdown as there was no possible means to conduct exams.

In chapter twenty, titled "Lockdown Funeral" the protocols associated with the Covid Funeral are mentioned. The protagonist here is a very rich person and it doesn't become a matter of thing to the pandemic; as death equalizes everyone in front of it and the bodies should be cremated electronically and no other means of method cannot be agreed by the Covid protocols. Also, not more than twenty persons were not allowed for the funeral.

Next, in chapter twenty-one "A Whiff of Eternity" the consumption of alcohol and anti-depressant pills can be seen in the character Shalu for getting relief from the stress and to maintain mental peace as she had haunting memories of her past relationship and feels distracted in everything she does. We can also see the mentioning of the fashion industry in the pandemic and how the mask which had been initially only meant for protection and no fancy had become a style statement by the making and usage of designer masks along with the purpose of protection. This chapter also talks about the importance and need of emergency medical funds as anyone can get infected by the virus anytime soon and everyone can't access the government hospitals as the hospital beds there had already run out completely.

In the chapter, twenty-two "Miss La Di Da" we can see the narrator being getting fed up with the home-schooling of his kid and how he had to manage his parents and the kid at the same time. As it was an online schooling method during the Lockdown he need to always check his son's home works and to ensure whether the digital setups are made properly for the online class. From this, we can see how much the parents especially, those who have work-from-home jobs have to balance everything along with kids schooling, their work deadlines, and home chores too.

In chapter twenty-three, "A Quest Ends" we can see the lockdown activities of a privileged couple. They have everything except a child. They had spent their lockdown time wisely by learning new things online. They had also found a solution for their long-time problem of being childless even after trying different methods to conceive. Finally, they came across the decision to adopt a kid. This chapter ends on a positive note.

In chapter twenty-four, "Open Letter to a Microbe" we can see a girl child who is praying and requesting the Corona Virus to go away as it had troubled so many people in different ways. The girl is telling that she and her friends had lost their beautiful moments of being together by celebrating birthdays, exchanging gifts, etc. we can see how the kids have fed up with home-schooling and how much they long for the reunion. The characters in this text always live with hope even in their worst conditions.

CONCLUSION

We had so far, analysed the impact of Lockdown and the Covid 19 Pandemic through the text *Lockdown Liaisons* by Shobhaa De and realised how lockdown and Pandemic had affected the lives of people and how they had tried to overcome it. We had also seen different types of people, with different attitudes, and their living conditions and how they face the pandemic with struggles, etc. Therefore, the pandemic and lockdown which could make us hopeless forever are healed by the process of reading literature especially through the works which had been written at that time.

WORKS CITED

De, Shobhaa. *Lockdown Liaisons.* Simon & Schuster India, 2020.

Festival, Jaipur Literature, "Shobhaa De: Lockdown Liaisons: Shobhaa De in conversation with Anandita De" YouTube, 24 Jun.2020,www.youtube.com/watch?v=4CmAotoxBww. Accessed 7 Dec.2020

"Lockdown Declared Word of 2020 by Collins Dictionary." *Financial Express*, 10 Nov. 2020, www.financialexpress.com/lifestyle/lockdown-declared-word-of-2020-by-collins-dictionary/2125618/. Accessed 9 Dec. 2020.

www.ingramcontent.com/pod-product-compliance
Ingram Content Group UK Ltd.
Pitfield, Milton Keynes, MK11 3LW, UK
UKHW040007200726
13854UKWH00001B/84

9 798885 466585